LONDON'S STREET TREES

Paul Wood arrived in London in the 1990s, having grown up on the chalk in Dover, and after graduating from art school in Cardiff.

Paul lives in well-forested Islington. He is the author of *London is a Forest* (2019) and *London Tree Walks* (2020), and the editor of *Great Trees of London Map* (2020). He continues to photograph and write about trees and urban nature on *thestreettree.com*. Follow him on social media as *@TheStreetTree*.

A large Caucasian Wingnut grows at the end of his street.

Fodor's ESSE

Publisher: Stephen I
Manager

Editorial: Douglas
Jill Fergus, Jacir,
Sadlowski, *Seni*
Alexis Kelly, R

Design: Tina M
and Productio
Designer; Mar
Production In

Production: Je
Production N
Production E
Editor

Maps: Rebe
Stroud (M
Lindroth, I

Writ

Edi

LONDON'S STREET TREES

A FIELD GUIDE TO THE URBAN FOREST

Paul Wood

SAFE HAVEN

For Katherine, who still likes trees

First published 2017 by Safe Haven Books Ltd
12 Chinnocks Wharf
42 Narrow Street
London E14 8DJ

This expanded and revised edition published 2020.

www.safehavenbooks.co.uk

A catalogue record for this book is available from the British Library.

ISBN 978 1 916045330

10 9 8 7 6 5 4 3 2

The Safe Haven team on *London's Street Trees*:
Paul Wood, Graham Coster

Designed by paulwoodcreative.co.uk
Set in Meta Serif Pro and Priori Sans

Printed and bound in the EU by Graphy Cems

It is *not* safe to eat fruit, berries or nuts from any London street tree. Please do not pick them, either.

Right: Chinese Red Birch, Giesbach Road, Archway

Page 1: Heart-shaped London Plane, New Cross Road

Pages 2-3: Kelfield Gardens, North Kensington

Page 7: View of London from Severndroog Castle, Shooters Hill

ACKNOWLEDGEMENTS

I am hugely grateful and indebted to all the people who have given up their time, walked round the streets of London with me, and offered their help in any number of ways. Particularly these people:

Scott Barkwith	Anne Jaluzot	Bruce Saunders
Rupert Bentley Walls	Mark Johnston	Gordon Scorer
Ben Brace	Michael J Keane	Melanie Sharp
Peter Coles	Trina Lynksey	Al Smith
Chris Colwell	John Medhurst	Jefferson Smith
Robin Crookshank Hilton	Stephen Middleton	Vincent Stops
Marie-Claire Denyer	Xanthe Mosley	Andrew Stuck
Simon Edwards	Moira O'Donnell	Oliver Stutter
Peter Fiennes	Greg Packman	Mel Sutton
Mick Finch	Tim Peters	Harry Thacker
Mathew Frith	Steve Pocock	Jake Tibbetts
Alison Gowman	Katrina Ramsey	Susan Unwin
Patrick Hegarty	Keith Sacre	David Welch

My special thanks to Mathew Frith, Director of Conservation at the London Wildlife Trust, for all his help, and for the content of the fact box about wildlife on page 45.

And all the people on Twitter and Instagram who have helped with tricky identifications and provided tip-offs on tree locations.

Any errors are mine.

RARITY RATING

A rarity rating for each species of tree on London's streets is given by the number of Plane leaves. (This does not take into account further specimens in parks or gardens.)

🍁🍁🍁🍁🍁 Very Common

🍁🍁🍁🍁☆ Common

🍁🍁🍁☆☆ Infrequent, but may be locally common

🍁🍁☆☆☆ Occasional

🍁☆☆☆☆ Rare

CONTENTS

Foreword 9

Introduction 10

What Trees Grow in London? 12

Mimosa or Silver Wattle 14

Pimlico's Australian Connection 16

Feijoa or Pineapple Guava 18

The Maples 20

Field Maple 22

Norway Maple 24

Sycamore 26

What Were the First London Street Trees? 28

The Horse Chestnuts & Buckeyes 30

Horse Chestnut 32

Tree of Heaven 34

Radical Street Tree Planting in Bermondsey 36

Persian Silk Tree 38

The Alders 40

Italian Alder 42

What Have London's Street Trees Ever
    Done for Wildlife? 44

The Juneberries or Snowy Mespils 46

Strawberry Tree 48

Where Do London Street Trees Come From? 50

The Birches 52

Silver Birch 54

Himalayan Birch 56

Hornbeam 58

Sweet Chestnut 60

Indian Bean Tree or Catalpa 62

Sheffield: a Cautionary Tale 64

Nettle Tree 66

Judas Tree 68

Peanut Butter Tree 70

Cabbage Palm 72

The Dogwoods 74

Turkish Hazel 76

The Thorns 78

Paul's Scarlet Hawthorn 80

How Much is a London Street Tree Worth? 82

Handkerchief or Dove Tree 84

Bragania or Erect Crab Apple 86

Beech 88

An Open-top Bus Tour of London with
    a Difference 90

More Ashes 92

Raywood Ash 94

Ginkgo 96

Honey Locust 98

Hibiscus 100

Who Plants London's Street Trees? 102

Willow-leaved Sandthorn 104

Golden Rain Tree 106

Do Different London Boroughs Have
    Different Street Trees? 108

Crêpe Myrtle 110

Chinese Tree Privet 112
American Sweetgum 114
Tulip Tree 116
The Magnolias 118
The Ornamental Apples 122
Why Pollard the Trees? 126
Dawn Redwood 128
The Mulberries 130
Olive 132
Hop Hornbeam 134
Persian Ironwood 136
Foxglove or Princess Tree 138
The Pines 140
An Oasis of New Zealand in Vauxhall 142
London Plane 144
Oriental Plane 148
What Does the Future Hold for London's Planes? . . . 150
The Poplars 152
The Flowering Cherries 154
London's Hanami? 158
London's Street Trees in Art 160
Caucasian Wingnut 164
The Ornamental Pears 166
Chanticleer Pear 168
The Oaks 170
English Oak 172
False Acacia or Black Locust 174
Giant Redwood 176

What Street Trees Doesn't London Have... Yet? 178
Jacarandas in London? 180
The Willows 182
The Rowans and Whitebeams 184
Whitebeam 186
Rowan or Mountain Ash 188
Wild Service Tree 190
What Are the Great Street Trees of London? 192
Japanese Pagoda Tree 194
The Limes 196
Common Lime 198
The Elms 200
Japanese Zelkova or Keyaki 202
Four London Street Trees of the Future 204
London Street Tree Walks 206

1. North: An Archway Perambulation 208
2. South: Herne Hill Highlights 210
3. East: The Haggerston Hop 212
4. West: Steve's Chiswick Chase 214
5. West End: A Bloomsbury and Fitzrovia Jaunt 216
6. The City: A Square Mile Saunter 218

Index of Latin Names 220
Index of English Names 222
Further Reading and Picture Credits 224

FOREWORD: THE MAYOR OF LONDON

London is an incredible city, and our trees and green spaces help make our city such a fantastic place to live.

This book encourages you to stop and look up at the amazing trees on our streets. There are a huge variety of species out there to explore. Beyond the Plane trees, there are species from all over the world growing and thriving in London.

Paul's guide is full of history and fascinating facts about our city. I want Londoners to be inspired by the photos in this book to plant trees. As Mayor I'm proud to have overseen a major tree planting programme across London, which has resulted in hundreds of thousands of new trees being planted. Londoners, boroughs and businesses can all get involved in tree planting to ensure London remains one of the world's greenest cities.

Sadiq Khan
Mayor of London

INTRODUCTION

In 2017, when the first edition of this book was published, it was greeted as something of an outlier. Reviews were favourable, and plentiful – but slightly astonished, nevertheless, that an entire book could be written on the subject of street trees. A lot has happened since.

In that first edition, I calculated around 300 species and cultivars could be found on the streets of London. I have since discovered Hackney alone has over 350. And while that borough has the most remarkable and diverse collection of street trees in London, there are still species not present on its streets that can be found elsewhere: a smattering of Caucasian Wingnuts in Islington, at least one Catalina Ironwood in Chelsea and a handful of Cork Oaks in Southwark. 'What about Willows?' wrote a reader from Hampstead soon after the book came out. This edition includes the Weeping Willows of Greenland Water.

Not only does this new edition include more tree species, but I have also had three years to photograph the urban forest, and to finally do justice to its colourful splendour.

Today, I'm confident there are over 400 types of tree lining high streets, boulevards, avenues and closes across this great green city. New species like the Peanut Butter Tree have appeared on them, and who'd have expected to find Persimmons, or Pecans? Pines have become more plentiful, too. Next, I can predict with conviction, will be the first Lemon tree on a London street.

But just as the number of species has increased (a decade from now I would not be surprised to count upwards of 500 species and cultivars), so has Londoners' interest in them. What began as the novel idea of one or two guided walks to inspect the street trees around

various independent bookshops from Dulwich to Hampstead is now, nearly three years later, a regular activity: many spring, summer and autumn weekends I find myself leading tree walks, and I've published a whole book of them with Safe Haven. Above all, as I report on page 102, Londoners are raising funds to plant their own streets with resplendent species like Persian Silk Tree, a species much admired in the pages of this book.

This diversity is relatively new. A century ago, A. D. Webster wrote in 'London Trees' that 'nothing very remarkable is to be found in the way of street trees in London.' Sixty per cent, he estimated, were London

of change in the urban forest is rapid. The humble Field Maple, the glamorous American Sweetgum and the rare Paper Mulberry thrive in what appear pretty unfavourable conditions.

Of earlier species like poplars, by contrast, only aged examples of these magnificent billowing trees can be seen on the street. The attractive, fast-growing Tree of Heaven was once commonplace in places like Bermondsey, but its propensity to jump ship and opportunistically take up residence wherever it can has made urban foresters less keen on what was once considered a wonder tree. But as the looming climate emergency makes the benefits of trees in cities more obvious, one of the most remarkable, and hopeful, things I've noticed is just how fast trees can grow on London's streets. In just a few years, a vulnerable sapling can transform itself into a confident adult tree.

Then again, since this book first came out – Sheffield happened (see page 64). Campaigners had to fight a long battle to save hundreds of magnificent, mature street trees from the axe. It shows, I think, just how much we value our urban trees, and how far we are prepared to go to protect them.

Street trees reflect the aspirations of a city, the conditions of the present and our legacy for the future. In London, grand oaks and planes offer a direct connection with the glories and inequalities of its past; exotic Olives and Crêpe Myrtles celebrate our multicultural world city as well as its changing climate, while Tulip Trees, Dawn Redwoods and Ginkgos will grace our streets for generations to come. I hope you enjoy discovering them all.

Planes, then the height of arboreal fashion. Now, it's only around 3%. But that is because the overall number and diversity of trees has increased dramatically, not because we have lost thousands of Planes. So, to Webster's generation, and those before him, we owe a debt of gratitude for the mature giants that now define this city, and the very desire to plant street trees at all. It was only fifty years earlier that the first street trees were systematically planted along the Embankment. Now it would be hard to imagine London, or indeed any city, without them.

We could think of the last 150 years as a great experiment, and one we are still engaged in. The pace

Above: Carr Road, Walthamstow: a typical tree-lined London street

WHAT TREES GROW IN LONDON?

Trees do well in London. With its remarkable diversity of species from all corners of the world, the capital is something of an arboreal sweet spot. Our frequent rain and mild winters, coupled with the urban-heat-island effect that raises temperatures above those of the surrounding countryside, enable trees to thrive that might shiver in colder continental winters. Familiar native and European species have been joined by exotic strains from Asia, the Americas and Australasia, to the extent that it's difficult to imagine what might once have grown here.

But when London was no more than a bend in the river, the landscape would have been very different.

The capital's geography is characterised by a broad, clay river basin, surrounded by higher chalk hills to the north, west and south. The Thames of old meandered through Oak and Hornbeam woodlands more slowly than today's embanked river flows through the modern metropolis. On flood plains, and where tributaries joined the Thames, Willow, Alder and Black Poplar were once common.

As London became settled, forests were cleared and the landscape became dominated by farming. At the dawn of the 19th century the city embarked on its biggest growth spurt, and between 1831 and 1925 became the largest city in the world, and the one we know today.

Despite centuries of growth, destruction and

mentions for two rarities: the riverside giant, Black Poplar, and a woodland curiosity, the Wild Service Tree. We would do well to consider planting these species more frequently.

As a port, a great trading city and formerly the centre of an empire, it is not surprising that London has been the gateway for waves of arboreal immigrants that have made their mark on the city's treescape. Early settlers from Europe included Sycamore, Sweet and Horse Chestnut and, originating in Spain, the London Plane.

Then came North Americans like Tulip Tree and False Acacia, followed by Asian species including Tree of Heaven and Golden Rain Tree. Still they come – the intriguing Dawn Redwood didn't arrive until after the Second World War. The nursery industry is now global: trees growing on our streets are usually cultivars especially developed for urban situations, and many will have started life in nurseries overseas.

In this botanical melting-pot it is inevitable that species go native, and the few parts of undeveloped London show what an urban forest might look like if it was left to its own devices. Just like the story of human migration to this city, a railway cutting near my home is home to a range of native and non-native tree species living cheek-by-jowl. Ash, Oak and Hawthorn are part of a diverse flora including Norway Maple, Eucalyptus, Apple, Loquat, False Acacia, Turkish Hazel and Tree of Heaven.

reconstruction, faint echoes of an ancient landscape can still be traced through woodland remnants such as Epping Forest, Oxleas and Coldfall Woods, and place names like Poplar, Honor Oak, Seven Sisters, Penge and Nine Elms.

The most recent swathe of London to be developed, the south-east, was once covered by the Great North Wood, an area of forest and wood pasture stretching from Deptford to Croydon. It is in bosky Norwood and Forest Hill that isolated relics of this landscape can be glimpsed in parks, gardens and even the occasional street.

So it is the mighty English Oak and the elegant European Hornbeam that we should consider as London's heritage trees, with perhaps honourable

Opposite: Hornbeam coppice, uncut for perhaps a century, creates deep shade in Coldfall Wood, East Finchley

Above left: Old Oak trees, once woodland or boundary trees and now street trees, line Oaks Road, Croydon

MIMOSA OR SILVER WATTLE

Acacia dealbata 🍁☆☆☆☆

The winter-flowering Antipodean tree found in Pimlico, Vauxhall, Mayfair, Peckham and Stoke Newington.

Originating from southern Australia and Tasmania, Mimosa was introduced to these shores in 1820. Commonly planted in London's parks and gardens, it is unusual as a street tree. Surprisingly exotic, almost tropical, this acacia is a welcome addition to the urban forest, particularly on a grey February afternoon, when it is likely to be one of the few trees in flower.

In its native habitat, Mimosa is a pioneer species, with similar characteristics to alder or birch in northern Europe: it likes disturbed soils, it is fast-growing but short-lived, and it does not tolerate shade from larger, more slow-growing trees.

I first came across flowering Mimosa street trees one gloomy winter day in Shoreditch. Not only was I dazzled by the abundant yellow blooms, but their sweet, floral perfume also cut through the usual urban aromas. Long admired by perfumers, Mimosa is a constituent of bottled fragrances by the likes of Givenchy and Gucci.

I have since discovered other trees gracing pavements and roadsides from Peckham to Stoke Newington. So far, though, I have yet to see systematic planting, which could be transformative on streets brave enough to host them.

One notable specimen blocks Moreton Terrace from joining Lupus Street in Pimlico. In shape, height and suitability this tree shows all the potential the species offers, in an uncompromising position entirely surrounded by paved surfaces, with a busy road alongside. It could be an ideal tree for other London streets afflicted by reflected heat, heavy traffic and inner-city pollution.

Apart from a relatively short lifespan – Mimosas do not survive for longer than about 40 years, so halve that for a street tree – the Achilles heel for this species is freezing temperatures. Any lower than -5°C and frostbite can kick in, potentially killing young trees completely, so this is a tree for urban heat islands where larger trees would not work.

I look forward to visiting a real Acacia Avenue one day...

ANOTHER AUSTRALIAN ON LONDON'S STREETS

Australia is known for gum trees, and thirsty eucalypts with the potential to become enormous may occasionally be seen on London's streets. This Tasmanian Cider Gum (*Eucalyptus gunnii*), resides on Druid Street, SE1.

Above right: A stunning mature tree, Lupus Street, Pimlico

Below right: The distinctive feathery foliage of Mimosa, seen opposite the Connaught Hotel, Carlos Place, Mayfair

Below far right: Sweet-scented yellow flowers in February on the corner of Carden and Forester Roads, Peckham

PIMLICO'S AUSTRALIAN CONNECTION

The Australian Mimosa just pictured announces a street lined with even more exotic antipodean trees. Moreton Place in Pimlico must be the only street in London lined with *Callistemon citrinus*, or Bottle-brush trees.

These strange, gangly, small trees – an unkind person might describe them as bushes – are native to eastern Australia, where they are found in areas with a cool, moist climate, not unlike London. The Pimlico trees flower from June to October, and it is quite a sight: brilliant red flower spikes, in distinct bristles that give the tree its name.

How did they come to be growing in a stuccoed Regency terrace? Number 7 has the clue: a blue plaque commemorating Australia's, coincidentally seventh, prime minister, Billy Hughes, born here in 1862.

Pimlico was planned in 1825 as a southern extension to Belgravia. At this time street trees were not in fashion; instead, garden squares like Warwick and St George's were the thing. Consequently, the street trees in this corner of Wesminster are a largely 21st century innovation and the species here reflect contemporary tastes. Ginkgoes, fastigiate Oaks, Raywood Ash and Japanese Pagoda Trees grace the terraces, along with that Westminster favourite, the neatly conical (and overplanted) Chanticleer Pear.

By the time of Hughes' birth in 1862, 40-year-old Planes would be hanging over the squares, but it would be another decade before London started planting roadside trees.

Hughes emigrated to Australia as a young man, and became one of its longest-serving prime ministers. A colourful figure, he was Australia's disputatious representative at the 1919 Paris Conference that signed the Versailles treaty after the First World War, the first international agreement Australia signed. He also crashed his car crossing the Sydney-Melbourne railway while taking his second wife on a 'long drive' instead of a honeymoon. Perhaps he was distracted by a Bottlebrush tree.

So it seems (though the Westminster Council representative I spoke to insisted it was pure coincidence) that these Australian trees were planted in honour of a famous Australian, a precedent I would love to see adopted for other London streets. Perhaps we could have Almonds or Cypresses on Hackford Street in Lambeth, where Vincent Van Gogh stayed in 1874 – or American Sweetgums in Tedworth Square, Chelsea, where Mark Twain resided in 1896?

Left: Number 7 Moreton Place and the blue plaque commemorating Billy Hughes

Right: A Bottlebrush tree in full flower on Moreton Place during early summer

FEIJOA or PINEAPPLE GUAVA

Acca sellowiana 🍁✩✩✩✩

The surprising Brazilian adding epicurean interest to Clapton, Shoreditch and Holloway.

With a name like Pineapple Guava, expectations are going to be high. Piña colada by the pool, anyone? So an initial once-over of this small, somewhat untidy tree might be underwhelming. But look a little closer, and you may be surprised.

In the summer, hidden among the leathery deep green leaves with their silvery undersides, striking flowers lurk. In isolation, these pudgy red and white blooms are quite remarkable. The only way I can think to describe them is as pumped-up plasticky Fuchsia flowers. Chunky white petals surround an array of red filaments ending with white anthers. Those fleshy petals ensure these blooms are edible, and are, so I'm told, quite delicious. I have yet to try one, but they allegedly impart a sweet, cinnamony taste. This may explain why you have to look so closely to find them.

The flowers that do manage to avoid the attention of either birds with exotic tastes or reckless urban foragers will, by November, have grown into rather unobtrusive fruits. These are the feijoas, a delicacy enjoyed in much of Latin America and now grown commercially in France and New Zealand. The fruits resemble a very short cucumber, roughly the same hue as the evergreen leaves, and they can be markedly abundant on the trees I know.

So if the flowers taste of cinnamon, are the fruits where the Pineapple Guava name comes from? Not far from a Holloway tree, an independent greengrocer with an extraordinary range of fruit and veg occasionally stocks 'Finest Colombian Feijoa'. An opportunity not to be missed, but at £2.00 a pop, an infrequent one. Eaten like a Kiwi fruit, the pale yellow-green flesh is scooped out from the skin, and is... interesting. The fruit is perfumed, akin to a guava, but even with a bit of imagination, pineapple eluded me. The texture is slightly gritty, again rather like guava, and the taste is sweet in a rather, well, plasticky way.

This is a street tree for the curious, and one that is likely to remain rare.

WHY ARE THERE SO MANY NON-NATIVE STREET TREES?

Many people ask why we don't plant more native tree species on our streets. There are several good reasons for planting trees from other parts of the world. They may be better suited to the man-made climate of the city, and of course they might be able to thrive among the traffic, Tarmac and pollution better than natives. I think they make the city considerably more interesting too. But we should keep planting natives as well, as they provide more benefits to wildlife.

Opposite: Flowers on a tree on Rivington Street, Shoreditch

Above: Feijoa fruits on a tree outside the Landseer pub, Landseer Road, Holloway

Right: A young tree on Lancell Street, Stoke Newington

THE MAPLES

Acer spp. 🍁🍁🍁🍁🍁

Like Londoners, the maples, or *Acers*, are a diverse lot, with hundreds of species. At least a dozen can be seen on our streets, along with many more cultivars.

All maples have similar winged seeds or samara, the helicopters that spiral gently to the ground in autumn. Beyond this, they are variable, with all shapes and sizes, different leaf shapes and bark. Maples occur naturally all over the northern hemisphere, from Europe and Asia to North America.

The staple urban maple at one time would have been the Sycamore (*A. pseudoplatanus*), but over the decades, more have been introduced, with Silver (*A. saccharinum*) and Norway maples (*A. platanoides*) being much favoured during the twentieth century.

During the twenty-first century, maple diversity has increased dramatically, and London now boasts representatives of the genus from around the world. Three of the most frequent species and their cultivars are discussed over the following pages, but for the

Acer enthusiast here's a taste of some of the species that have either fallen out of fashion, or are on the start of their planting ascendency.

Trident Maple (*A. buergarianum*), is certainly a species in the latter category. Newly planted specimens of this Asian tree – so called for its three-pronged leaves – have started to appear around town. Another distinctive Asian species occasionally encountered is the distinctive **Paper-bark Maple** (*A. griseum*). It is a small tree with deep-reddish brown bark peeling in translucent strips and has compound leaves composed of three distinct leaflets.

The so-called snakebark maples, all characterised by attractive veined bark that must once have reminded someone of snakeskin, are another intriguing group of maples. You might find **Père David's** (*A. davidii*), an attractive species that would be nice to see more of on our streets.

Silver Maple is a tree very much out of fashion. A large North American named for its silvery-white leaf undersides, it is frequent, but newly planted specimens are almost non-existent. Many have been pollarded and often quite badly, so perhaps its planting champions of the 70s and 80s didn't realise quite how large they might become.

Of the other maples, the east Asian **Amur Maple** (*A. ginnala*), is one of my favourites. Small and slow-growing, it can look rather messy when young, but patient dwellers of Amur Maple-lined streets can expect an attractive if somewhat gnarled specimen to emerge after about 20 years. It could be mistaken for a large hawthorn but, as with all maples, the samara will give away its true identity.

If all these aren't enough, you might also see the

suckering **Cappadocian Maple** (*A. cappadocicum*), with a distinct red cast to its bark and young shoots. **Box Elder** (*A. negundo*) is present in some boroughs: another maple with compound leaves, it is best in early spring when its flowers appear.

Perhaps the maple most frequently planted currently is **Freeman's** (*A. x freemanii*). A hybrid between Silver and **Red** (*A. rubrum*) Maples, which could be mistaken for Sycamore, Freeman's comes into its own in October with fine autumn colours.

But so far **Sugar Maple** (*A. saccharum*), the source of maple syrup, hasn't made it...

Far left: Leaves and samara of an unusual Trident Maple outside Haggerston Overground Station

Left: Leaves and samara of an Amur Maple outside Herne Hill Station

Above: A well-managed Silver Maple billows in Bounds Green

Right: Female flowers of a North American Box Elder, Victoria Road, Stroud Green

FIELD MAPLE

Acer campestre 🍁🍁🍁🍁☆

A hardy native maple found all over town from Balham to Willesden Green.

Field Maples can cope with a lot. I especially admire a tree on the Hornsey Road in north London which typifies the street-tree population. Drunks lean against it, powerfully-jawed dogs are tethered to it, buses brush past it, a cocktail of Thunderbird, 7 Up and worse is frequently fed to it. Despite all this tender, loving care the tree is doing just fine.

Easily identifiable by its small-by-maple-standard leaves and corky bark, a mature Field Maple maintains a neat medium size – another reason for the species' popularity. The only truly native British maple, it can be found growing in hedges, at the edge of woods, and as a coppiced woodland tree. It is commonest in southern England where it thrives on well-drained chalk soils.

So London is well within its range and, despite our city soils being on the whole neutral clays, Field Maple thrives here too, and is rightly popular among urban foresters. Most Londoners, therefore, are likely to be no more than a few minutes away from a neighbourly Field Maple.

Nurserymen saw in this unassuming tree a winning formula, and have been tweaking it for at least a couple of centuries, developing scores of cultivars, many of which are popular street trees today.

Unlike the familiar Beech tree, which has a very distinctive cultivar in the Copper Beech, Field Maple cultivars are subtle, tending to focus on shape rather than leaf characteristics. Those likely to be encountered include **'Arends'**, with a regular oval crown, **'Red Shine'**, with subtly reddish leaves, and the slender, conical **'Queen Elizabeth'**.

WHAT IS A STREET TREE CULTIVAR?

Cultivars are named and recognised tree varieties cloned in various ways to maintain distinct, consistent features such as variegated leaves, an upright habit or particularly dense branches. They are products of the horticultural industry and, while some are developed for their suitability to withstand urban conditions, others are all about an attractive feature. An example of a cultivar is the Raywood Ash (*Fraxinus angustifolia* **'Raywood'**), see page 94. It has stunning autumn foliage but is structurally weak, so both these good and bad features are preserved through clonal reproduction.

Left: Young leaves and developing samara on the front-line Hornsey Road tree, on the 91 bus route to Crouch End near Archway

Above: Fine autumn colour displayed on a Buchan Road, Nunhead, tree

Right: A newly planted specimen on Snowsfields outside Guy's Hospital

NORWAY MAPLE

Acer platanoides 🍁🍁🍁🍁🍁

This good-looking Scandinavian is found across town from Wimbledon to Abbey Wood.

One of the most commonly planted street trees throughout London, Norway Maple is a handsome species, at first glance difficult to tell apart from the Sycamore, with which is has much in common: similar leaves, similar sizes and similar native distribution.

The differences are subtle. Norway's leaves are spikier, and its flowers in spring are held in distinctive fresh green clusters. Sycamore, on the other hand, produces a long, pendulous flower spike. Norway's bark is light-coloured and grooved, Sycamore's darker and scalier.

The charms of large maples have not been lost on the horticulture industry, which has developed myriad cultivars. Look out for Norway Maples of various leaf colour from gold through to deep purple; for fastigiate trees (with upward sweeping branches) and neat round trees, as well as an intriguing variegated (speckled-leafed) variety. Significantly, Norways are able to tolerate many different soils, extremes of temperature, air pollution and drought, and so are a popular choice for the urban frontline.

Although Norwegian by name, *Acer platanoides* is native to much of Europe, including Belgium and France. If it wasn't for post-Ice-Age sea-level rises, a few additional centuries of continental connection might have seen this species arriving under its own steam in what is now eastern Britain. As it is, the cultivation of Norway Maple can be dated back to 1683. No doubt ornamental planting over the centuries has played a part in its naturalisation, and now Norway Maples thrive and regenerate freely in our climate.

I welcome them.

A NORWAY MAPLE DESIGNED TO CONFUSE

'Palmitifidum' is the name of this rarely seen cultivar with deeply incised leaves. A row of four can be inspected on Eldon Road, Walthamstow.

Top right: Flowers appearing on a purple-leaved **'Royal Red'** cultivar in the central reservation of Dog Kennel Hill, East Dulwich

Centre right: A golden foliaged cultivar of **'Princeton Gold'** on Downham Road, De Beauvoir Town

Bottom right: A variegated **'Drummondii'** cultivar, a form where some branches show variegation while others do not. Seen on Wilberforce Road, Highbury

Far right: A handsome round-domed tree on Hartswood Road, White City

SYCAMORE

Acer pseudoplatanus 🍁🍁🍁🍁🍁

The common-or-garden tree found in all parts of London from Acton to Woodford.

As trees go, this one is controversial. Though arguably the maple most familiar to most Londoners – commuters may recognise it from suburban railway embankments where, along with Buddleia, Sycamore is a key component of the trackside flora – the Sycamore is considered by many to be non-native.

Some arboreal fundamentalists go so far as to brand it an invasive species. Sycamores reproduce with gay abandon, as their copious seedlings in early spring will testify, and such fecundity is perceived to be a threat to more abstinent native species seemingly unable to compete.

But there is a counter-argument: this is a large, familiar tree with an important role in our landscapes. Sycamore may not appear in prehistoric pollen records, but its arrival on British shores is an undateable, mysterious event, and we should embrace its honorary native status. Indeed in northern parts of Britain, Sycamore takes on the landscape role that Oaks do in southern parts. One landmark tree marks a breach in Hadrian's Wall known as 'Sycamore Gap'.

Interesting, then, that it should be a London street tree, for while splendid examples can be seen in many parks and gardens, here Sycamore's vulnerabilities are exposed. Our streets and pavements can reflect too much heat and are not as moist as it would like. It certainly tries hard, but Sycamore street trees tend to be relatively weedy, unlike Norway Maple.

As with other maples, several cultivars exist, and tend to make up the bulk of London's street tree population. Those most likely to be be encountered are on either the variegated or purple-leaved ends of the spectrum. Unlike many street trees, cultivars developed for form – fastigiate for instance – do not seem to exist or are avoided by street planters. Look out for variegated **'Leopoldii'**, or **'Spaethii'** with dirty purple leaf undersides which can be quite nasty.

In my opinion the original Sycamore is still the best, and when mature can be a handsome street tree.

A LOVELY SYCAMORE FOR THE SPRING

Of all the Sycamores cultivars, **'Brillantissimum'**, with delicate pinky-yellow spring leaves, is perhaps the most attractive.

Top right: This fine mature Sycamore is something of a local landmark outside Hornsey Town Hall in Crouch End

Below right: Sycamore leaves in Clapham, less spiky than the even more frequent Norway Maple

Far right: A lowering **'Spaethii'** cultivar on Highbury Hill near Arsenal Tube station

WHAT WERE THE FIRST LONDON STREET TREES?

London was late to street trees. It was Georges-Eugène Haussmann who, in his wholescale renovation of Paris that began in 1853, pioneered magnificent tree-lined boulevards, and set the style for grand urban design in Europe.

In London, the very first street trees to be systematically planted were London Planes, lining the Victoria Embankment, whose construction was completed by Joseph Bazalgette in 1870 – as they do to this day.

Berkeley Square, of course, was already well known for its huge Planes dating back to 1789; Brunswick Square too, while the central London parks remain great places to see Planes in their full glory.

Though London seems full of Plane trees, it might be surprising to learn that only 4% of the trees in inner London, and just 1.4% of trees in the whole of Greater London, are Planes. But a trend had been set. By the end of the 19th century, street-tree planting had become routine.

Inevitably, there was a class element in the street trees planted on London's new residential streets. An account of late-19th-century planting in Camberwell notes that large trees including Planes and Horse Chestnuts were favoured for wide, villa-lined avenues, while it was 'Limes, Laburnums and Acacias for the middle-incomes; unadorned macadam for the wage-earners'.

By the beginning of the 20th century, new housing was being built all over town, with street trees now expected in such developments. The commonest species were Plane, Lime, Poplar, Horse Chestnut and False Acacia or Black Locust – all large trees, and often inappropriate in the long term for anything other than a broad boulevard.

By the time A. D. Webster was writing his book on *London's Trees* after the First World War, Tree of Heaven had joined the list, but in 1920, he estimates, 60% of street trees were still Planes.

But other street trees were starting to appear: Webster lists Silver Birch, Sycamore, Bird Cherry, *Pyrus* (pear trees, but at this time rowans and whitebeams were classified as *Pyrus*), Almond and something tantalisingly called Dwarf Acacia, which may be the now unusual **'Umbraculifera'** cultivar of False Acacia. Sweet Chestnut, willows, hawthorns and elms were occasionally planted too.

By the 1930s birches had become popular, and many inter-war streets were lined with graceful Silver Birches. Fast-forward to the post-war years and such species were still popular, but perhaps with greater emphasis on smaller flowering trees like thorns, rowan and whitebeams.

As postwar regeneration took hold London re-planted in fits and starts, and the legacy of experimentation can be seen in some boroughs: mature Golden Rain Trees in Hounslow, Caucasian Wingnut in Islington, for instance. With the redevelopment of the former docklands in the 80s and 90s, new species became popular: more maples, especially Silver and Norway and their cultivars.

But there remain many streets across London without street trees. Hackney has only recently made up for lost time by planting a plethora of trees along the borough's streets, while Lewisham, Newham, and Dagenham and Redbridge have a great many streets without trees.

London's Mayor, Sadiq Khan, came to power pledging to plant many new trees during his time in office. We are beginning to see more trees in some boroughs; however, the austerity of recent years has meant street trees are often a low priority for local authorities juggling diminished budgets.

Perhaps, though, the biggest issue for street trees is not their numbers but their size: the smaller the species of tree, the less the maintenance. But it is the mature, expansive canopy of big trees rather than the number of saplings that offers Londoners the most environmental benefits.

As the climate moves up the political agenda, street trees may be seen as part of the solution. Could this mean we start to see larger species planted, and even new avenues of Planes?

I hope so.

Left: Claude Monet's 1871 painting of 'The Thames Below Westminster' features a young London Plane

Right: An Edwardian postcard shows the newly completed, and planted, Windermere Road in Muswell Hill

THE HORSE CHESTNUTS & BUCKEYES

Aesculus spp. 🍁🍁🍁🍁🍁

We call them Horse Chestnuts because their large woody nuts are inedible, only good for horses perhaps, unlike delicious sweet chestnuts, which are borne by trees of a completely different genus.

In North America, species of the *Aesculus* genus are known as Buckeyes, their dark glossy brown nuts resembling the eyes of deer. However, most of the trees encountered on London streets are of European or Asian origin, and are known as Horse Chestnuts. All have distinctive five-lobed, or palmate, leaves, showy flower candles and seeds that ripen within pods, but only the seeds of European Horse Chestnut are good enough for a game of conkers.

Unlike that species (described on the following pages), other Horse Chestnuts are less susceptible to unsightly leaf miner attacks, and are therefore favoured for new planting. Melbourne Grove in East Dulwich is a great place to see all the species mentioned here.

The most commonly planted of the 'other' Horse Chestnuts is **Red Horse Chestnut** (*A. x carnea*), a tree which has been popular for decades, so mature examples are fairly common. A cross between the European Horse Chestnut and the North American Red Buckeye, it flowers at the same time as, and is sometimes planted together with, the regular Horse Chestnut. Like many hybrids, it is sterile so, alas, no conkers. Of several cultivars, **'Briotii'** offers the deepest magenta flower colour.

A very occasional street tree with yellow flowers is the American **Yellow Buckeye** (*A. flava*); an elegant smaller tree with rounder chestnuts. A very safe and boring game of conkers could, at a pinch, be played with the seeds of this and another occasional London street tree, the Indian Horse Chestnut.

Don't let those inferior chestnuts put you off though; the **Indian Horse Chestnut** (*A. indica*) is a magnificent tree which deserves to be more frequent. Like a more elegant version of the European Horse Chestnut, it is a little smaller and has more delicate leaves. The key to its identification is flowers appearing in late June, well after its European counterpart's. Particularly lovely when little else of its size and stature is flowering.

Left: A mature Red Horse Chestnut in full flower on the Stroud Green Road, Finsbury Park

Above: An Indian Horse Chestnut on the corner of St George's Drive and Denbigh Street, Pimlico

Right: Ripe chestnut of an Indian Horse Chestnut in late October on a Kendall Street, Paddington, tree

HORSE CHESTNUT

Aesculus hippocastanum 🍁🍁🍁☆☆

The familiar and much-loved conker tree found in East Dulwich and all over town.

As a kid, I had a mental map of all the local conker trees, ready for the autumnal race against time to collect as many as possible for endless games of bashing your opponent's wooden-fruit-on-a-string with your own until one of them shattered. We were happy with simple pleasures in those days. But nowadays, come October, my neighbourhood streets are littered with unclaimed fruits.

Originating from the Balkans, Horse Chestnuts were an early introduction here in the 17th century, and are common especially around London's outer boroughs, as large individual specimens and in mature avenues. Many substantial street trees may be remnants of Victorian or Edwardian gardens left in situ as the city grew and adopted into the streetscape.

Horse chestnuts have a lot more going for them than just conkers. They're big, handsome trees with large, unusual and easily recognisable leaves: the horseshoe-shaped wound the leaf stems leave when they fall in the autumn gives rise to the equine name.

The flowers are something special, too. Appearing in May, flower spikes, or candles, consist of up to 50 individual white flowers which on closer inspection each show a pink spot. When Horse Chestnuts first arrived here people must have been amazed by such a remarkable tree.

Sadly, Horse Chestnuts are now rarely planted, for two reasons. The first is their large eventual size, the second the pathogens now visibly affecting this species. The most obvious of these is the larva of a leaf-mining moth which from mid-July causes the tree's leaves to wilt and die.

This afflicts nearly every specimen in London but, despite its unsightliness, trees survive without it affecting flowering or conker production. It surely must weaken the trees over time, allowing another problem, a fungal infection known as bleeding canker, to take hold. This is less obvious, but far more serious and can cause trees to die. One to watch out for.

AN UNUSUAL DOUBLE-FLOWERED HORSE CHESTNUT

· ·

A cultivar occasionally encountered is Bauman's or Sterile Horse Chestnut (*A. hippocastanum* **'Baumanii'**). It has double flowers that produce no conkers, so is of use to neither man nor bees, and is consequently rare!

Top: A fresh glossy conker below a magnificent tree on Haslemere Road, Crouch End

Above: Leaves and flowers of a tree in Walthamstow

Right: Melbourne Grove in East Dulwich is lined with many fine Horse Chestnuts of various species and cultivars

TREE OF HEAVEN

Ailanthus altissima 🍁 🍁 ☆ ☆ ☆

The 'Ghetto Palm', found in Bermondsey, Lambeth, Barnsbury and Stepney.

Tree of Heaven, introduced from China in the late 18th century, quickly became popular during a time when anything 'Chinoiserie' was the height of fashion. As its suckering tendencies became apparent there was then a pause in planting until the later 19th century, when its suitability as a pollution-proof street tree for industrial London was recognised.

Seemingly impervious to smoke and fumes, by the early 20th century Tree of Heaven was one of the most commonly planted trees in London, together with Plane, Lime and Poplar. It was deemed even more resilient than Plane, and recommended for planting in the 'smokier districts' of south and east London.

Being a relatively short-lived tree – most last for less than 70 years – Tree of Heaven is now much less visible than the Plane, but large specimens can still be seen, notably in Lambeth and Southwark, lining streets like Long Lane in the Borough.

A relatively easy tree to recognise throughout the year, Tree of Heaven has distinctive patterned bark and pinnate leaves (multiple leaflets on a single stalk). Resembling giant Ash leaves, they are probably the largest of any street tree, and can reach 60-70 cm long even on young trees.

Swaying in the breeze, these exotic-looking leaves, which on male trees smell like old trainers, coupled with the species' vigorous reproductive habit, gave rise to several popular names including Tree of Hell and, in New York, the Ghetto Palm.

In London I have seen no newly planted street trees, but many new arrivals sprouting from cracks in the pavement, railway embankments and other 'edge lands'. Along with its ability to grow happily in the poorest of soils and survive extremes of drought and heat, this tenacity illustrates some of its attraction for early urban foresters.

While doing all this, though, Tree of Heaven also chemically poisons other plants in the vicinity, to ensure its own dominance.

So it's a tree of two halves. On one hand it is a large, graceful tree, disease-resistant and able to take most of the things London throws at it. On the other, it has hordes of unruly children, bad BO, and kills its neighbours. On balance, not a good thing to have on these honest streets.

Right above: A self-sown Tree of Heaven grove on the corner of Battersea Park Road and Kirtling Street

Right below: Seeds developing in September on a Hemingford Way, Barnsbury tree

Far right: A mature tree on Marchmont Street, Bloomsbury

Before 1965 and the streamlining of local government, London was made up of a multitude of small
boroughs, the boundaries of which can sometimes
just about be traced, thanks to the street-tree-
planting decisions made decades ago.

Nowhere is this more evident than in the Tree of
Heaven-lined streets of the former borough of
Bermondsey, once one of the most deprived areas of
London, with notorious slums housing workers from
the warehouses, tanneries and docks that stretched
from London Bridge to Surrey Quays.

At the beginning of the last century a young
couple with a strong sense of social justice, Ada and
Alfred Salter, made their home in Bermondsey among
the poor and needy.

He was a brilliant doctor who set about adminis-
tering to the distressed and disease-ridden slum
dwellers; she, a committed Quaker and Christian
Socialist, got stuck into social reform, trade unions
and radical politics.

Eventually Ada Salter became Mayor of Bermondsey – no mean feat back in 1922 – and thus the first
female mayor in London, and the first female Labour
mayor in the country.

During this period mayors were relatively powerful, and Ada used her position to demolish and
redevelop the worst of the Bermondsey slums and
generally improve the borough's environment. She set
up the Beautification Committee, which by 1930 had

succeeded in planting over 7,000 trees.

In a borough then so densely populated that in 1921 120,000 people lived there (by 1961 it was just 51,000), the Committee managed to plant trees on 70 of the borough's 80 miles of roadway. Many can still be seen today.

Ada's favourite was the Tree of Heaven, and it was with this species the Beautification Committee pioneered the planting of around Bermondsey. At the time the species' controversial invasiveness must not have been apparent – or perhaps back then it simply didn't reproduce to the extent it can now in what may be a fractionally warmer climate.

Though individual specimens can survive for up to 100 years, less than 70 is more common in urban locations, so today many are reaching the end of their lives, but there is nowhere better than Bermondsey and Rotherhithe to see fine mature examples of this street tree, and through them trace the borders of a vanished borough.

As the trees in Southwark are replaced, but not with Tree of Heaven, these relics of social history will diminish, but Ada Salter's pioneering work lives on through a memorial garden in Southwark Park, a statue on Bermondsey Wall East, and a young Tree of Heaven (perhaps the first deliberately planted in London for decades) with a corresponding plaque, in Bermondsey Spa Gardens.

Left: A fine example of a Tree of Heaven in the Alfred Salter Playground in Bermondsey marks the vault where the Salters' ashes are interred

Above right: The statue of Ada Salter, complete with spade, on Bermondsey Wall East

Below right: Plaque in Bermondsey Spa Gardens remembering the councillors of Bermondsey who lined the streets with Tree of Heaven

TREE OF HEAVEN
(Ailanthus **altissima**)

This tree is dedicated to the Bermondsey Councillors of old who lined the streets with the Tree of Heaven to ease the effects of poverty on health and the quality of life : and to the working - class communities of the Borough who withstood much hardship with great fortitude. Others, both here and abroad, were to follow the Councillors' initiative.

" **They who plant trees love others besides themselves.** "

PERSIAN SILK TREE

Albizia julibrissin 🍃☆☆☆☆

A real head-turner seen in Brockley, Nunhead, Dulwich and Stoke Newington

In flower, this tree is a stunner. Feathery pink blooms, sometimes in great profusion, dust the canopy from July and keep on going through to October.

When it's not in flower, the delicate foliage resembles that of Mimosa (see page 14); leaves are bi-pinnate, meaning they split twice, so a single leaf might be composed of hundreds of tiny leaflets. Unlike Mimosa, Persian Silk trees are deciduous, and in winter they become just another leafless tree, the only inkling of their summer glory might be a few shrivelled leguminous (or pea-like) seed pods.

Although its name is Persian, *Albizia's* natural range spreads throughout Asia east to the Korean peninsula. But, as with many plants, its names, both English and Latin, commemorate where it was originally introduced from, and by whom, in this case by a member of the Florentine Albizzi family. Albizzi's 18th-century imports came from what's now Iran, where Silk Trees are a constituent of the Caspian Hyrcanian Forest, a strip of species-rich woodland bordering the southern Caspian Sea. This fertile forest is also the original home of other scarce London street trees, including the Caucasian Wingnut (page 164) and Persian Ironwood (page 136).

In the US, Persian Silk Trees have been popular for decades, their exotic leaves and flowers proving irresistible to gardeners and urban foresters from New York to Florida. But, as with many planting fads, the consequences have been predictable, and Silk Trees have gone feral and are now listed as a 'weed of concern' by the US Forestry Service. Could this be a lesson we should heed? Even a slight temperature increase here might lead to a plant like the Persian Silk Tree striking out from its urban niche like Buddleia before it.

This is one of the reasons why I appreciate the rarity of this tree. But, if it were more frequent, it might be taken for granted, an overplanted ornamental whose interest would certainly wane with familiarity. Planted thoughtfully and sparingly, though, Persian Silk Trees have the ability to thrill Londoners for generations to come. Having said that, a whole avenue would be quite stunning!

Left: Flowers composed of 'silken threads' on Dulwich Village's landmark tree outside the Crown and Greyhound

Right: A tree in full flower, Nevill Road, Stoke Newington

Far right: One of several newly planted trees outside Brockley Station

SHOULD I LET MY DOG PEE ON A STREET TREE?

No! It may seem like a time-honoured tradition for dogs to cock a leg against a street tree, and indeed many old trees seem to be none the worse from decades of canine interest. But young trees can be chemically poisoned by too much dog, or indeed any other mammal's, pee. So keep your pooch on a tight lead around young street trees – they have plenty of other problems to deal with already!

THE ALDERS

Alnus spp. 🍁🍁🍁☆☆

Alders are a confusing bunch. They have cones in winter like a conifer, and one particular cultivar has leaves like a conifer too.

Alders are monoecious, meaning trees have both male and female flowers. The gender differences are pronounced, with male catkins conspicuously long, and female catkins usually smaller and developing into distinctive cones which disperse tiny winged seeds.

These cone-like structures, specific to alders, stay on trees through the winter. And in this season you would be forgiven for thinking you had stumbled across a deciduous conifer such as the increasingly planted Dawn Redwood (see page 128), so look out for the catkins, which will reveal its true identity.

Our own native alder, the **European or Black Alder** (*A. glutinosa*) is present on our streets, along with two interesting and attractive cultivars, both very different from the regular species.

'**Imperialis**' and '**Laciniata**' both have incised leaves bearing little resemblance to the blunt-leaved species or indeed other alders. '**Laciniata**' resembles something between a hawthorn and an oak, while '**Imperialis**' has leaves so deeply cut and feathery it looks more like a conifer.

A promising alder which we are likely to see more in coming years is the hybrid **Spaeth's** (*A. x spaethii*). It is a cross between Italian and Japanese Alders and is slightly more appealing than its Italian parent, described on the following pages, with which it shares much in vigour and shape. Spaeth's has a distinctively-shaped leaf, more like a cherry's, which can cause problems with identification, so look for the cones!

The other alder that may be seen is the drab-sounding, and indeed drab-looking **Grey Alder** (*A. incana*): look out for it in supermarket car parks and other prime spots . That said, Grey Alder does have an attractive cultivar in *A. incana* '**Aurea**' or **Golden Alder**. Some boroughs, Haringey for instance, seem to be keen on it, so head to north London in the winter to see its striking yellow branches and pink male catkins, followed by gold-ish foliage.

Far left: Interesting leaves of an **'Imperialis'** cultivar on the corner of Alma and Scotland Green Roads, Enfield

Above left: Cherry-like leaves of a Spaeth's Alder on Cheapside in the City

Above top: Leaves of a **'Laciniata'** Alder on Upper Street across the road from Angel Tube station

Above: A young Golden Alder on Victoria Terrace, Finsbury Park

Right: A tough European Alder on Wembley Way

ITALIAN ALDER

Alnus cordata 🍁 🍁 🍁 ☆ ☆

The utility tree, often seen in the centre of town, including Westminster and the City.

The Italian Alder is a fast-growing, large and slender tree. It requires little maintenance, and is consequently a straightforward choice where height is wanted but space is limited.

Unlike our native Alder (*A. glutinosa*), which requires damp ground, the more glossy Italian thrives in most London locations and can tolerate a lot of abuse, including poor soil, pollution, heat and drought. In fact, this species appears to like London so much that seedlings can commonly be found shooting up in gardens near to street trees.

All the alders are known as pioneer trees, and are quite happy even in the poorest soils where few other trees can thrive. They are able to take nitrogen from the air and fix it in the soil through a symbiotic relationship with bacteria. In the wild, this can enrich soils, enabling other species to grow in their wake. In other words, alders are doing the groundwork for future forests.

This capability could be useful in the capital, too: in central London particularly, centuries of development and demolition have left the soil (or substrate, in the jargon) little more than rubble.

On the face of it, Italian Alders have a great deal going for them: they keep their leaves well into December, they clearly have a love of London, and they make a useful contribution to improving soil.

Aesthetically, Italian Alders are great in late January and early February when the yellow male catkins appear. But at other times of the year they are not the most interesting of trees. I wonder if they could be considered overplanted?

WHICH STREET TREES ARE BAD FOR ALLERGY SUFFERERS?

Trees producing wind-blown pollen are the worst offenders as far as allergy sufferers are concerned. Tiny male pollen particles are easily breathed in by humans. Alders and Birches can really get up peoples noses along with Ginkgo, Oak, Hornbeam and Sweetgum. Plane trees are irritating in May, reducing some to tears. Trees with insect-pollinated flowers like Cherry or Rowan are much safer bets.

Left: A tall and narrow tree on Broadway opposite St James's Park Tube station

Above: Heart-shaped leaves and developing female catkins, Pancras Road, Somers Town

Right: A large tree in full flower during February on the corner of Bessborough and Rampayne Streets in Pimlico

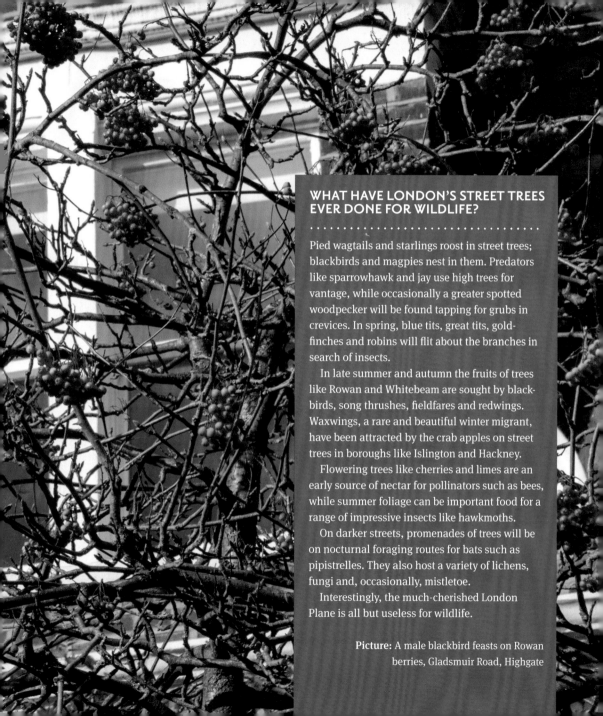

WHAT HAVE LONDON'S STREET TREES EVER DONE FOR WILDLIFE?

Pied wagtails and starlings roost in street trees; blackbirds and magpies nest in them. Predators like sparrowhawk and jay use high trees for vantage, while occasionally a greater spotted woodpecker will be found tapping for grubs in crevices. In spring, blue tits, great tits, goldfinches and robins will flit about the branches in search of insects.

In late summer and autumn the fruits of trees like Rowan and Whitebeam are sought by blackbirds, song thrushes, fieldfares and redwings. Waxwings, a rare and beautiful winter migrant, have been attracted by the crab apples on street trees in boroughs like Islington and Hackney.

Flowering trees like cherries and limes are an early source of nectar for pollinators such as bees, while summer foliage can be important food for a range of impressive insects like hawkmoths.

On darker streets, promenades of trees will be on nocturnal foraging routes for bats such as pipistrelles. They also host a variety of lichens, fungi and, occasionally, mistletoe.

Interestingly, the much-cherished London Plane is all but useless for wildlife.

Picture: A male blackbird feasts on Rowan berries, Gladsmuir Road, Highgate

THE JUNEBERRIES OR SNOWY MESPILS

Amelanchier spp. 🍁🍁☆☆☆

The North American tree with an identity crisis, found all over town from Camberwell to Croydon.

Variously known as Serviceberry, Snowy Mespil and Shadbush, the Juneberries have over the last decade become some of London's most popular street trees, so chances are you are just a few streets away from one.

Most examples are small, and many are the **'Robin Hill'** cultivar – another name to complicate matters. Confusion extends to Latin names, too. There are several variants that even botanists struggle to tell apart, but *A. arborea*, *A. lamarckii* and *A. laevis* may be encountered. What these little trees lack in lack of identity, they make up for with fabulous spring blossom, not to mention a fiery autumn display.

Juneberries burst into flower in April at the same time as some cherries, and can be mistaken for them. Flowers are accompanied by bronze-coloured new leaves, making them both striking and distinctive, if only fleetingly. The leaves and bark of Juneberries are quite different from a cherry's: the bark is smooth grey with a faint vein pattern, and the leaves are small and delicate and might be described as slightly oblong. Tiny apple-like fruits appear in June and are much sought after by birds. They're apparently delicious; consequently, they don't last long.

At the other end of the year, Juneberries' autumn colours, especially on trees exposed to full sun, can be stunning. Leaves develop a red tinge to their edges which over a couple of weeks bleeds into the full leaf. The overall effect is striking, with some leaves deep scarlet, others more orange, and there's usually a flash of green too.

Now, back to names... Since Juneberries already have so many other names, and are now so widely planted, I think the time has come for Londoners to drop this rather dull, if accurate, moniker in favour of something far more resonant. I like Shadbush, but this is no mere bush – so let's go the whole hog and call it Shad Tree. This is redolent of those London peculiars, Shadwell in the East End and Shad Thames, that picturesque street (not as yet lined with *Amelanchiers*) running parallel to the Thames south of Tower Bridge.

Above: Autumn leaves can turn a spectacular red, like these on Nightingale Lane tree in Hornsey

Right: Berries appearing in June on a Fawnbrake Avenue tree in Herne Hill

Far right: A young tree shows the spring blossom potential for this species on Trinder Road, Crouch Hill

WHAT HAPPENS TO THE TIMBER WHEN STREET TREES ARE CUT DOWN?

· ·

When the inevitable happens, most ex-London street trees end up as wood chip, which has lots of uses for things like biofuel and garden mulch. But one man, Bruce Saunders, has recognised what an amazing resource London timber can be for furniture makers and wood turners. Saunders Seasonings acquires large trees, putting the timber through the mill and seasoning it for up to two years.

After this long process, prime London Plane wood – also known as Lacewood – can change hands for anything up to £2,800 per m³. Plane tree timber is exceptionally good, along with oak, elm and walnut, but Bruce says Norway Maple wood can be stunning too.

STRAWBERRY TREE

Arbutus unedo

The evergreen Irish tree with simultaneous flowers and fruits, found in Bermondsey, Vauxhall, and Haggerston.

I was surprised, even a little excited, when, on a Southwark street way back in 2011, I discovered a row of newly planted Strawberry Trees.

As an unusual child with an interest in native trees, I had known the Strawberry Tree even then to be a fascinating and mysterious species with an alluring name. It is famously native to south-west Ireland, notably the Killarney National Park, where it appears to have clung on during the last ice age. Otherwise this tree is confined to south west Europe.

The English name may arise from the appearance of the fruits – dimpled and bright red – but Strawberry Trees are actually related to the heathers, a kinship more apparent in their white, bell-shaped flowers. A lovely feature is the simultaneous flowering and fruiting in the autumn. The fruits themselves take 12 months to ripen, going through every hue from lime green to vermillion.

The tree's botanical name, *unedo*, is derived from the Latin phrase *unum edo*, 'I eat one', which for this cautious author says it all.

Characterised in the wild by bushy growth, Strawberry street trees have been raised to produce 2 metres of straight trunk before their unruly characteristics are allowed free rein. They promise to make interesting street trees, providing year-round shade and colour.

Those specimens I came upon line Melior Street, a short turning behind London Bridge in the shadow of the Shard. After nearly ten years, a few have gone missing, but several remain and are doing just fine. Never a constituent of the post-glacial Bermondsey forest, or marsh, the Strawberry Tree, with its evergreen foliage and drupe-like berries, confers an unexpected lushness on its adoptive environment.

Subsequently I have encountered examples elsewhere in Southwark, and in Islington and Hackney. Special mention must go to Arbutus Street, off the Kingsland Road in Dalston, where a thoughtful urban forester has planted two examples of this tree. Which came first, though: the trees or the street?

Left: Arbutus Street is behind Haggerston Station

Right above: The fruits of the Strawberry Tree are at their best in October

Far right: One of the Southwark trees outside the Horseshoe Inn, Melior Street, behind London Bridge Station

A RARER STRAWBERRY TREE

Unusual **Hybrid Strawberry Trees**
(*A. x andrachnoides*) are well worth
looking out for in high summer.
The orange outer bark peels to
reveal green new growth. See one
in Bonnington Square, Vauxhall or
Guthrie Street, Chelsea.

WHERE DO LONDON STREET TREES COME FROM?

Ever since humans started to plant trees, we have also needed to propagate them, in order to have a ready supply for our gardens, orchards and woodlands. The task of selecting and supplying trees from the forest for our varied needs – food, timber, but also beauty – has often fallen to dedicated nurserymen. Over the centuries, nurseries have not only grown trees, but also imported, grafted and 'improved' them through selective breeding, giving rise to today's global horticultural industry.

Until the second half of the 20th century, some London boroughs had their own tree nurseries, where trees would be raised for planting in the local streets and parks. In Southwark, a legacy of the former borough of Camberwell, a council-run nursery in Honor Oak next to Camberwell New Cemetery was supplying trees, shrubs and flowers for civic planting right up until the 1980s.

Several factors have led to the demise of local authority nurseries: spending cuts, political will, increasing land values and the growth of the city's horticultural requirements have all made growing trees in London unviable.

Nowadays, all London boroughs buy their trees from commercial growers, something many boroughs have always done. You may notice on newly planted street trees nursery labels, giving the species' name and also the nursery's name. There are several suppliers of street trees, including Hillier Trees, Majestic

Trees and others, but the one that appears to supply the majority of London's street trees is Barcham Trees.

I was kindly shown around Barchams' nursery by their Sales Director, Keith Sacre. It's a vast operation, spread over many acres of Cambridgeshire fenland, with row after row of trees lined up in plastic containers ready for packing off to the frontline. Barchams' business is not confined to street trees, or indeed London: they provide trees for gardeners, landscapers and urban foresters across the country.

The scale of the operation is also reflected in the size of the range. Barchams' catalogue boasts over 300 tree varieties, including 43 different cherry trees alone. During the planting season from October to March, they will shift hundreds, if not thousands of trees every day.

And what about prices? Not all street trees are equal. At the bargain end of the range, common species like Rowan or Silver Birch might cost around £150 each, while a showstopper such as a Handkerchief Tree would be more like £500. These prices reflect things like demand and ease of propagation.

At the moment Himalayan Birch is popular, but, as we will see, fashions change unpredictably. A nursery could suddenly be left with a lot of unwanted trees on its hands. Paul's Scarlet Hawthorn and Whitebeam have been popular in the past, but now there is much less demand for them.

So do the nurseries propagate all the trees, and if so how do they know that what they plant today will

be what their customers want in 5 to 10 years' time when the trees are big enough for shipping? Nurseries certainly do grow some trees themselves, but in order to supply what their customers want, they also buy in trees from growers as far afield as Italy and Germany.

In order to ensure pests and diseases don't arrive, however, or at least don't get out into the wild, biosecurity is now a crucial component of what nurseries offer. At Barchams, imported trees are kept in quarantine for a full year before they are put on sale, ensuring any potential nasties are picked up and eradicated.

Opposite: Barcham Trees' nursery in Cambridgeshire

Left: A nursery label on a newly planted Himalayan Birch on Milton Park, Highgate

Above: A 'Spire' Cherry (*Prunus x hillieri* **'Spire'**), originally developed by Hillier's nursery in the 1930s on the Hornsey Road, Upper Holloway

THE BIRCHES

Betula spp. ★★★★☆

A varied bunch, all the birches are medium deciduous trees with more or less peeling bark. They are undoubtedly attractive trees, and most do well as street trees.

Birches live fast and die young: they are pioneer trees that opportunistically colonise disturbed ground. In the wild this means landslips, storm-damaged areas or forest edges. They're also known for covering swathes of the Arctic across Canada, Scandinavia and Russia. So life on London's streets must be well within their comfort zone.

Of course, not all birches are Arctic dwellers, and a surprising number can be seen around town. Silver and Himalayan Birch are the most common species and they're described on the following pages. Here, then, are some of the more unusual species.

River Birch (*B. nigra*) is a distinctive and handsome North American easily recognisable by its copiously peeling bark, a dramatic sight when first

encountered. Widely but thinly planted specimens tend to be mature, suggesting it has been out of favour in recent years. It deserves to be more widely planted again, and judging by a few recent sightings it may become more frequent.

Another unusual birch very infrequently seen is the Japanese **Monarch Birch** (*B. maximowicziana*). It is perhaps the least birch-like birch, with dark reddish-grey bark pitted, cherry-like, with lenticels (the horizontal marks often seen on the trunks of *Prunus* species). It has large un-birchy, cordate, or heart-shaped, leaves turning bright yellow in the autumn too.

Most people think of birches as having white bark, and the other species you may see all do – at least, they do eventually. **Chinese Red Birch** (*B. albosinensis*) trees develop dazzling white bark as

they mature, but, just to confuse, young trees have or-angey-brown bark. Most are the cultivar **'Fascination'**, distinguished from the very similar Himalayan Birch by that peeling brown bark featuring on younger branches even of mature trees.

Erman's Birch (*B. ermanii*) is another Asian species, again with white bark, although it tends to be less pristine and flakier. If you're unsure which birch you have, come back in October to see if the leaves are beginning to go golden. If they are, chances are it's an Erman's – it's always the first to turn in the autumn.

Other birches may be seen too. **Paper Birch** (*B. papyrifera*), the most common North American birch, is occasionally planted as a street tree. Also known as Canoe Birch, it was traditionally used by Native Americans for that purpose. **Downy Birch** (*B. pubescens*), is a native, and similar to Silver Birch, but with a more upright and rounded habit. Finally, **Sichuan Birch** (*B. szechuanica*) is another white-barked tree very occasionally seen.

Left below: Bark of a Monarch Birch on Hawksley Road, Stoke Newington

Left above: River Birch, Finsbury Park Road

Above: Erman's Birch on Braxfield Road, Brockley

Right: Peeling bark, **'Fascination'** Chinese Red Birch, Cranley Gardens, Muswell Hill

SILVER BIRCH

Betula pendula 🍁🍁🍁🍁✩

A graceful tree, found in Wanstead, Gospel Oak, West Norwood, Balham and beyond.

One of our commonest native trees, Silver Birch pops up in a remarkable variety of locations, from post-industrial brownfield sites to wind- and rain-lashed Scottish mountainsides. As a pioneer species, it loves difficult, nutrient-poor environments, and such built-in hardiness enables it to thrive on London's streets.

During the 1920s and 1930s, Silver Birch was a popular street tree, and occasionally large specimens from this early wave of planting can be found on quiet leafy avenues, although as Silver Birches rarely live longer than 80 years these sentinels will become increasingly unusual.

As we have seen on previous pages, several exotic birch species now vie for our attention, most with similar bark colouring and small leaves. Therefore, it is worth looking in more detail at the essential Silver Birch characteristics. It has silver, or more accurately white, bark, but then so do other birches; some are even brighter, and cleaner, though, so look out for black warty markings, especially around the base of the trunk on older trees.

Perhaps the easiest way to identify Silver Birch is by the graceful, weeping young growth peculiar to this species, which also gives us its Latin name, '*pendula*'. This characteristic means it is relatively easy to spot whatever the season.

A useful, attractive native tree that we ought to see more of, Silver Birch is, I think, preferable to some of the exotic birches now popular. There are a few cultivars to look out for and two in particular are very occasionally found on our streets:

'**Purpurea**', a purple-leafed form, is a strange wispy tree. It is slow-growing and slender, and may not be the ideal street tree for every situation,

'**Youngii**', or **Young's Weeping Birch**, is a rather hunched, weeping tree often associated with neatly clipped suburban front gardens, but does very occasionally make it street-side too. An odd choice.

SWEDEN'S NATIONAL TREE

Ornäs Birch, also known by the cultivar name **'Dalecarlica'**, is the national tree of Sweden. It was originally discovered during the 18th century in central Sweden, and every specimen is a clone, by now many times removed, of that original tree. It is widely planted, and can easily be identified by its distinctive, deeply incised leaves. This one is on Stamford Brook Road.

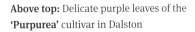

Above top: Delicate purple leaves of the **'Purpurea'** cultivar in Dalston

Above: Typical warty bark of a mature tree on Clapham Common Southside

Right: Middle-aged tree on Windermere Road, Muswell Hill, possibly of the **'Tristis'** cultivar

HIMALAYAN BIRCH

Betula utilis var. jacquemontii 🍁🍁🍁🍁🍁

The new kid on the block, found all over town from Tooting to Finchley.

Chances are the nearest birch to you is this one. '*Betula utilis jacquemontii*' is the phrase on many an urban forester's lips when it's time to order a new street tree. Otherwise known as the Himalayan Birch, it is the tree of the moment, and newly planted specimens can be found on highways everywhere. If trees can capture the imagination, then this is a contender admired by both tree planters and residents across London.

What makes this tree so special is its remarkable, sparkling white bark, which can appear pristine even on a wet and gloomy day.

Himalayan Birch was first brought to Europe in the late 19th century from Nepal, India and Tibet, and until its recent raising to arboreal high-fashion status was a relatively rare and obscure tree mostly found in botanical collections.

The variety name '*jacquemontii*' arises from 19th-century botanical confusion: initial specimens were thought to be a separate species (*B. jacquemontii*), but were later proved to be a variety of the previously described *Betula utilis*, Himalayan Birch, hence the rather long-winded scientific name now in use.

This variety – a classification distinct from a sub-species – differs from the regular species, which can be more variable, with yellow, orange or brown bark.

In the wild the tree has for centuries been an important, yet sustainable, resource, its wood used for fuel, its leaves for animal fodder, and the bark as a kind of parchment for Kashmiri and Sanskrit religious texts. Sadly, the Himalayan Birch is now in trouble, owing to deforestation and over-use for fuel.

It's unusual for a single species to be 'discovered' and planted so rapidly, and it will be interesting to see how this tree thrives in London.

So far it appears to be coping well in most situations, but it's not known how long individual trees are likely to survive – some birches can be very short-lived. Nor do we know how large it might become. Will it even find London so like its native Himalayan slopes that it starts to propagate itself? Or will the vagaries of fashion mean we soon move onto another species and it suddenly seems like yesterday's tree?

Above: A young tree on Wild Court, Covent Garden

Right: Bark of a Nutbrook Street, Peckham tree

Far right: A winter tree dazzles, Kirby Grove, Bermondsey

WHY DO BIRCHES HAVE WHITE BARK?
. . . .

As pioneer species, Birches have evolved to cope with situations other seemingly more robust trees would find difficult. Given half a chance, they will colonise newly cleared ground, and it is in these environments that their white bark can come in useful. It may be cold on the south-facing slope of a Himalayan or Rocky Mountain peak in winter but, come the summer, the sun can be fierce. So a tree with reflective white bark in an exposed position has an advantage over species happier in a shady forest.

HORNBEAM

Carpinus betulus 🍁🍁🍁🍁☖

The true London tree – found right across London from Norwood and Dulwich to Harrow and Highgate.

London is slap-bang in the middle of the English Hornbeam belt: an area of woodland that once swept from Essex and Hertfordshire south through Middlesex to Kent and Sussex. The capital's remaining, very special, pockets of ancient woodland, including Oxleas Wood, Epping Forest, Coldfall and Highgate Woods, bear witness to this, with native Hornbeam still abundant. So Hornbeam has been thoroughly at home here for millennia, and it's no surprise that it also does well on our streets.

Many street trees are examples of the tidy pyramidal cultivars **'Fastigiata'** and **'Frans Fontaine'**: striking, tapered, crucible-shaped trees that make for great avenues. On a moonlit evening, a street lined with mature, wine-glass Hornbeams can be quite magical, evoking a nostalgic Metroland of tidy, tree-lined, safe suburbia. The non-cultivar species can also be encountered but, unfortunately, much less frequently. It is more subtle, a beautiful spreading tree requiring more space, but given its association with London should be more widely planted.

Another reason to plant more Hornbeams is their biodiversity value: they provide food and shelter for smaller, less obvious Londoners. A recent study showed that a City of London Hornbeam supported more living things than any other tree in the Square Mile. Some achievement, given there are oaks in the City too.

The name refers to its tough wood ('horn' being analogous to hard, and 'beam' an old English word for tree), hinted at perhaps in the musclebound appearance of mature tree trunks. The light-coloured wood is extremely hard and produces excellent charcoal, hence the frequency of old coppiced trees in those ancient woodland remnants. At one time, locally grown hornbeam would have been the fuel of choice for Londoners. The wood is hard-wearing too, and was much prized for everything from tools to butcher's blocks and, nowadays, furniture.

Could you be sitting on a decommissioned London street tree?

ANOTHER HORNBEAM

The elegant **Japanese Hornbeam**, or **Kuma-shide**, (*C. japonica*) is a rarely seen curiosity. It is notable for its elongated leaves with more prominent teeth than the European tree. London's few specimens – like this one on St Margaret's Road, Brockley – tend to be small. Our own Hornbeam is therefore unlikely to be overshadowed any time soon.

Above: Leaves and ripening nuts on a Swains Lane, Highgate tree

Right: A fine example of **'Fastigiata'** on Westwood Park, Forest Hill just beginning to show its autumn colour

SWEET CHESTNUT

Castanea sativa 🍂🍂🍂🍂🍂

The tasty tree: found in Islington, Hammersmith, Spitalfields and Kentish Town.

Sweet Chestnuts are unrelated to Horse Chestnuts (see page 30). Their nuts do have a passing resemblance, but their single, deeply toothed leaves are completely different.

Huge and ancient Sweet Chestnut trees can sometimes be seen in historic London parks and gardens – Greenwich Park is home to many astonishing veterans over 400 years old, planted at the behest of King Charles II and mentioned by Samuel Pepys.

The London street tree population is somewhat younger and smaller, but with the potential for greatness. A notable row graces the north side of Pentonville Road between King's Cross and the Angel. It's a brave choice – trees can live for centuries – and it can only be hoped these street trees will last as long as those in Greenwich. They are mostly doing well, but some on narrower streets elsewhere are looking less healthy. It will be interesting to see how the Pentonville row holds up in years to come.

Trees flower in July, and are again very different to those of its equine namesake. Held in copious creamy-coloured strands, they have a distinct aroma, likened by some to, er, semen.

Sweet Chestnuts are not native to the UK, but are described as an archaeophyte, meaning they were introduced before 1500 AD, probably by the Romans as a source of fast-growing timber. They respond to coppicing well, throwing up vigorous new growth, suggesting that street trees will be fine on a regular pruning and pollarding programme.

Although from the same species, nuts harvested from our street trees will not bear much resemblance to those sold by roasted-chestnut sellers at Christmas. London chestnuts usually hold multiple seeds, while varieties needed for stuffing or roasting produce just one nut per spiny case or cupule.

The primary harvest from British trees is timber, valued for being useable without seasoning. Formerly it was prized for making hop poles, but these days is used mostly for fencing.

Above: Developing chestnuts and typical saw-toothed leaves on a Rona Road, Gospel Oak tree

Right above: One of the Pentonville Road trees in full flower during July

Right below: October, and ripe chestnuts peep out from a fallen spiky cupule on Pentonville Road

WHICH TREES ARE BEST FOR BEES?

All trees produce flowers, some more conspicuously than others. Some flowers are wind-pollinated, while others require the services of insects to help with fertilisation. Sweet Chestnut has masses of flowers that are very attractive to bees. In chestnut-rich areas, particularly in southern Europe, chestnut honey can be harvested, a particularly dark and strong-tasting substance. But London's rich arboreal diversity ensures urban honey has a huge number of different flavourings.

INDIAN BEAN TREE OR CATALPA

Catalpa bignonioides 🍁🍁☆☆☆

The brash pop star tree, found in Kennington, Limehouse and Mayfair.

Southern Catalpas live fast and shine brightly. Also known as Indian Bean Tree, great specimens can occasionally be found gracing broad boulevards and street corners in some parts of London. Apart from its ultimate size – not huge – everything else about it is big, brash even; to be expected, perhaps, from a tree originating from the banks of the Missisippi in the American Deep South.

This tree likes to spread, and can be broader than it is high, giving its giant leaves a chance to soak up the sun. These leaves, which are some of the largest of any tree found on our streets, are delicate and, unusually, secrete nectar, the subtle aroma of which is not unpleasant.

Flowers, on the other hand, are odourless but visually stunning, particularly as they appear in July when little else in the urban forest canopy is blooming. Even a bad year is pretty spectacular, the trumpet-like flowers opening in clusters of up to 40 individuals. They appear white and frilly, but on closer inspection there are purple and yellow parts, too. And then there are the beans: seed pods ripening to dark brown, a striking look even in winter.

Introduced in 1726, the tree has been popular ever since. The Victorians recognised an ability to cope with the pollution of their time, and venerable old trees, now entering their twilight years, can be found in parks, squares and even outside Parliament dating from the late 19th century.

Apart from a bit of leaf mildew, trees appear more than happy with London conditions, although they prefer a grass verge to a hard pavement.

A CATALPA THAT'S ALL ABOUT FORM

A cultivar occasionally seen is **'Nana'**, a smaller tree with a dense, mop-headed crown. It's a short-lived curiosity that rarely flowers, and in winter it can have the feel of a tangled witch's broom. The one above can be seen outside Borough Church across the road from Borough Tube station.

Right above: A group of Southern Catalpas provide a dense shady canopy on a hot July day, Narrow Street, Limehouse

Right: Flowers and last year's seed pods on a Conduit Street, Mayfair tree

Far right: A tree developing beans in September, Linden Avenue, Kensal Rise

SHEFFIELD: A CAUTIONARY TALE

The South Yorkshire city of Sheffield is synonymous with heavy industry, but it is also one of the greenest cities in the UK: home to 4.5 million trees, 36,000 of them on its streets.

Sheffield hit the headlines in 2017 after Amey plc, a private contractor brought in by the City Council to 'upgrade' the streets, set about this upgrade by chopping down the trees lining them. What followed is a cautionary tale for anyone who cares about trees and the environment.

It took a while for the citizens of Sheffield to realise what was going on, but after whole avenues of mature limes, ashes and oaks had gone – with even a rare Huntingdon Elm facing the chainsaw –

it was clear. Perfectly healthy trees that made a huge contribution to the quality of life in the city were being felled. Residents grouped together to try and stop what they saw as this heartbreaking, never mind unnecessary, destruction.

All these condemned trees, responded the council, had been found to be Dangerous, Dead, Diseased, Dying, Damaging or 'Discriminatory'. (What does *that* mean?) Of course, they would be replaced with new saplings, and the city would eventually see a net increase in the number of street trees.

But for many of the axed trees, the reasons just didn't seem to stack up. For a century-old Lime on Chatsworth Road in the suburb of Dore it was 'Kerbs missing, unable to repair without tree damage'. Campaigners argued that sensitive pavement engineering could enable it to stay. Christened 'Duchess Lime', this tree became something of a celebrity, with her own Twitter account (*@DuchessLime*), but she still came down, along with many more large, healthy Limes on her street.

By winter 2016/17, protesters across the city were interposing themselves between the trees and the felling crews, who took to turning up before dawn to outwit the human shields. Trees on the hit-list had yellow ribbons tied to them (many still do), along with their CAVAT values (see page 82), to show the council not only their significant financial value, but also the huge environmental contribution that the new 'lollipops' would take decades to match. Campaigners found themselves with criminal convictions for defying injunctions against stopping what even the Environment Secretary, Michael Gove, condemned, after a visit to Sheffield, as 'environmental vandalism'.

In March 2018 – the day after Duchess Lime was felled – the huge public backlash, international opprobrium and, no doubt, escalating security costs saw Sheffield City Council and Amey pause their cutting programme. Now, engineering solutions are being

sought to enable trees to be accommodated, residents are being, perhaps grudgingly, consulted, and the original contracts have been made public, revealing that no fewer than 17,500 street trees were to have been replaced.

So, what lessons have we learned? Hopefully Sheffield has taught local authorities to be very careful when contracting out to private companies motivated by profit – who quite reasonably seek to minimise costs by eliminating the factors that make them increase. A street of saplings doesn't need pollarding like a street of majestic mature Limes. But allow that metric to decide a tree's fate and you have a row of stumps where once was a glorious bosky avenue.

But perhaps the most important thing to come out of Sheffield is the huge lengths city dwellers will go to to protect their street trees – proving just how much they love them.

Far left: Campaigners gathered under the mighty Chelsea Road Elm, eventually saved from the chainsaw

Left: A scene repeated hundreds of times across the city: an 80-100-year-old stump of a perfectly healthy tree

Above: The CAVAT value on Duchess Lime

NETTLE TREE

Celtis australis

The street tree of the future, found in Plumstead, Shepherd's Bush, Soho and the City.

Don't worry – it doesn't sting!

A species we are likely to see more of in the coming years, the Southern European Nettle Tree has been known in London for a long time, but in the past planted only very rarely. Now it has been identified as a perfect candidate to cope with climate change and the rigours of city life.

A neat, small-to-medium-sized tree with a broad, round crown, it is rather elegant in an understated way. For this reason it will work best in an avenue, or as a specimen tree where there's no competition.

There is a good example in the City: a single tree guarding the marooned tower of St Alban, Wood Street. The rest of this Wren church was destroyed in the Blitz: all that was left was the tower, which now stands alone on a stone and concrete island surrounded by Tarmac and high-rise buildings. The Nettle Tree sits, unfazed, at the end of this concrete canyon, south-facing and surrounded on three sides by heat-reflecting walls.

Things are stacking up in its favour, then: succeeds in poor soils; tolerates cool winters; loves hot weather; can deal with drought; reflected heat is not a problem; provides shade – and can cope with pollution, too. And it doesn't need much in the way of maintenance! This tree ticks a lot of boxes.

This might seem an unremarkable tree: it doesn't have showy flowers or fruit, and will be unfamiliar to most people. But it does have a strong purpose and, if planted thoughtfully, the Nettle Tree embodies what it takes to be an arboreal success in the city.

Above: Nettle-like leaves on an Argyll Street tree behind Oxford Circus Tube station

Right: Bournewood Road, Plumstead, is a consistent avenue of thriving Nettle Trees

JUDAS TREE

Cercis siliquastrum

The Biblical tree. Found in Bermondsey, Vauxhall, the City and Shoreditch.

The Judas Tree is so named for Judas Iscariot. It was from a branch of this species, legend has it, that, filled with remorse after betraying Christ, he chose to hang himself. Shamed in turn by having Judas hang from its branches, the tree turned its white flowers to red (deep pink, actually). Interestingly, among several cultivars, the most likely one to be encountered is the white-flowered '**Alba**', suggesting some trees may be getting over their shame.

Apparently the flowers are edible, and in the Levant they are used as a salad ingredient. The leaves can be distinct, usually cordate, or heart-shaped, or sometimes almost round, even, and have a lovely freshness when they emerge before the flowers. Seed pods tend to remain on trees over winter and can be very profuse. They can dampen the flower display by hanging on right through the spring too.

The Judas Tree has long been an occasional London street tree, and some good examples can be seen around town. It is unmistakeable in flower: its blooms are deep pink to magenta, pea-like in shape. Amazingly, they burst straight out of the trunk, as though this tree wants to flower so much it doesn't have enough branches to cope. In some years flowers can be more abundant than others, but, regardless of abundance, flowers still perform the same trunk trick.

A native of the eastern Mediterranean, it can be a common street tree in southern Europe, and is another tree we are likely to see more of. Having said that, it can become rather untidy, so on balance might not be the best tree for pavements, and would be better suited to a grass verge or roundabout.

A NORTH AMERICAN JUDAS TREE

Eastern Redbud (*C. canadensis*) is closely related to the Eurasian Judas Tree, but its '**Forest Pansy**' cultivar – a street tree growing in numbers – is all about the attractive orange, red and purple foliage. Flowers are less profuse and more discreet. See them on Leverton Street, Kentish Town or Middleton Road, Dalston

Right above: Pea-like flowers sprouting from the trunk of a Vauxhall Grove tree

Right below: A seed pod in the City on Aldermanbury

Far right: A tree in spring, Gresley Road, Highgate

PEANUT BUTTER TREE

Clerodendrum trichotomum 🍁☆☆☆☆

A fine-smelling tree, full of surprises, seen in Lambeth and Hackney.

Also known as the Harlequin Glorybower, this is a tree for all the senses. When it's in bloom, from high summer through to early autumn, masses of white flowers emit a glorious aroma which can often be smelt before the tree is clocked.

It is a densely foliaged, rather shaggy, small tree originating from east Asia. It may be familiar as a garden shrub but, like some others, the Strawberry Tree (see page 48), or Hibiscus (page 100), for instance, it has been raised to tree status by the horticultural industry. In the case of the Peanut Butter Tree I can only applaud this, as it's such a lovely and fascinating plant.

Those flowers and their sublime aroma, akin to a sophisticated designer perfume, are, unsurprisingly, a draw for hive-loads of bees. The flowers are followed by strange fruits quite unlike any others in the urban forest. A deep-pink star-shaped cushion surrounds a small globular berry which turns from white to blue, eventually becoming black. Often, berries of different hues might be seen on the same tree, reflecting the protracted flowering time and consequently long fertilisation window.

With all this going on, where does peanut butter come from? Well, one more thing about this tree guaranteed to surprise is that the leaves, when crushed, give off a powerful odour of peanut butter. It's not 'like' peanut butter, as, say some banana-flavoured drinks only have a vague similarity to an actual banana.

No, the leaves of a peanut butter tree smell *exactly* like peanut butter!

Above: The bee-friendly flowers of a tree on Fawnbrake Avenue, Herne Hill

Above right: A strange fruit – cushion, berry and all – on a Morning Lane, Hackney, tree

Far right: A young tree on Mentmore Terrace opposite London Fields Station. Note the reddish-brown fruit of a Bee-Bee Tree beyond (page 204)

HOW CAN STREET TREES HELP LONDON'S ECOLOGICAL RESILIENCE?

Ecological resistance is the term used by conservationists to describe how nature can naturally deal with pests and diseases through greater biodiversity – the different types of plants and animals. Street trees have a part to play: the greater the number of trees close together along a road the better. They act as 'stepping stones' for birds and invertebrates moving around the city while also moderating microclimates, which benefit a broad range of wildlife.

CABBAGE PALM

Cordyline australis 🍁☆☆☆☆

The seaside palm tree, seen in Woolwich and Vauxhall.

Nope, it's not a true palm tree, but these native New Zealanders do a fairly good impression, and one that has been fooling British holiday-makers for generations. Cabbage Trees, sorry, *Palms*, are much planted in Gulf Stream-warmed seaside towns from Plockton on the west coast of Scotland to Cornwall, where they are so abundant they are known as the 'Cornish Palm'.

Undeniably sub-tropical in appearance, Cabbage Trees are quite hardy, and occasionally put in an appearance on London's streets, bringing a lush, resort-like vibe to the likes of Woolwich. Perhaps their appearance in this corner of south-east London is a nod to the town's former naval associations.

As every fan of musical theatre knows, Cornwall is synonymous with pirates, and in my imagination it was these old sea dogs who, retiring to their home ports after years of marauding in the South Seas, brought home the Cabbage Tree as a reminder of those happy days. Since then, *Cordylines* have become a decorative horticultural mainstay, and dozens of cultivars, with an array of leaf colours from golden and variegated to, bizarrely, brown, can be seen in well-kept gardens everywhere.

But where does that 'Cabbage Tree' name come from? It was the first Europeans arriving in New Zealand who named the trees, which the Maori know as Ti Kouka. These colonists had undoubtedly observed how the indigenous people used the plant for a multitude of purposes, including for making rope as well as a food source. The rhizomatous roots and young heart leaves are consumed. Not having tasted it myself, I assume it is these leaves that are the cabbage-like part.

Cabbage trees are perhaps at their best when they flower: great plumes of scented small white flowers are produced during summer. In turn these lead to masses of small white berries, which can persist through the winter.

Then again, perhaps winter is the best time for them, as their evocative silhouettes remind us of warmer times to come...

A REAL PALM TREE

· ·

The **Chusan**, or **Chinese Windmill Palm** (*Trachycarpus fortunei*), is a true palm tree, but I know of only one example used as a street tree, in Bonnington Square, Vauxhall (see page 142).

Right: Small white berries on a tree in winter

Far right: Cabbage Palms line Plumstead Road in Woolwich

THE DOGWOODS

Cornus spp. 🍁✩✩✩✩

A varied bunch, seen in Hackney, with solitary outliers in Dulwich, Kings Cross, and unverified reports from Crystal Palace.

There are quite a few dogwoods, at least three species of which are present on London's – or perhaps more accurately – Hackney's streets. Dogwoods are all flowering trees that produce berries, but otherwise they have little in common.

Our native Common Dogwood (*C. sanguinea*) is a frequent shrub of woodland edges and motorway embankments. It is most conspicuous in winter, when its bright red stems enliven even the dullest stretch of the M25. If you have ever looked closely at this Dogwood during summer, you will notice curving leaf veins reflecting the outline of the leaf. This is the one characteristic all the Dogwoods share, and is the sure-fire way to tell if you are dealing with a *Cornus*.

Hackney has pioneered their planting (as it has with many other trees), and its experiments appear to have paid off.

My favourite is the **Cornelian Cherry** (*C. mas*), a continental species that has been seen in gardens for centuries. It makes a small tree at its best in February, when acid yellow flowers coat the craggy twigs. It's

not in the same league as Mimosa (see page 14), but it is certainly heart-gladdening. At the other end of the year, large red berries appear, which have various culinary uses, often involving booze.

Chinese Dogwood (*C. kousa*) is more usually spotted in glamorous gardens. It has abundant, show-off, four-petaled flowers. Those petals are technically bracts: the flowers are held in an inconspicuous bunch at their centre. There are several cultivars of this tree, most with white flowers, but some have pink edges. Chinese Dogwoods are also worth revisiting in the autumn, when their large red fruits appear, resembling an exaggerated comic raspberry.

The other Dogwood I have seen in one or two Hackney locations is the **Wedding Cake Tree** (*C. controversa*), and its attractive variegated cultivar **'Variegata'**. This is a finely structured tree that sprouts evenly placed horizontal branches, becoming smaller nearer to its top. They resemble the tiers of a traditional wedding cake – hence the name – particularly when erect bunches of white flowers add an icing-like quality. This may be the least likely Dogwood to become an established street tree, as it needs room to show off their fine structure, as well as sympathetic pruners to maintain it.

Left: Leaves of **'Vareigata'** Wedding Cake Tree, Gransden Avenue, Hackney

Right above: A regular Wedding Cake Tree, Chesholm Road, Stoke Newington

Right below: A Cornelian Cherry in flower, Palatine Road, Dalston

Far right: A young Chinese Dogwood in full flower, Stamford Hill

TURKISH HAZEL

Corylus colurna 🍁🍁🍁☆☆

The Ottoman turban tree can be found in Haringey, Croydon, Islington and Kensington and Chelsea.

If you're familiar with our shrubby, multi-stemmed, common native Hazel, Turkish Hazel will come as something of a surprise. Like a giant tree version, with similar leaves and catkins, it grows much, much larger – an unexpected characteristic, judging by some street plantings I've seen, which dwarf smaller rowans and cherries.

Turkish Hazel assumes a neat, conical outline, which comes into its own in groups or avenues that emphasise uniform size and shape. The nuts, too, are of note: the Ottoman Empire is brought to mind by fruits resembling a sultan's turban. Arranged in clusters of up to four, and much loved by urban squirrels, each small nut is enclosed by a broad band of exuberant shagginess.

These involucre, or open-nut casings become apparent in high summer on trees bearing fruits – not always an annual event. They're strange, green, fleshy growths, with Sputnik-like protuberances that become browner and woodier as the nuts ripen and fall.

Turkish Hazel naturally ranges from the Balkans through Anatolia to the Caucasus and northern Iran, a key breeding-ground for species suited to northern European cities like London – the particular rigours of urban street life are actually very similar to the stresses on trees growing in the mountains of south-east Europe and western Asia.

Turkish Hazel trees will cope with drought, frost, reflected heat, and flash-flooding to boot. Good examples can be seen in parts of Haringey, the gastronomic heart of north London's Turkish community – considerate urban forestry, perhaps?

Above: A fine conical tree with an atypical bending trunk, Moray Road, Finsbury Park

Right top: Catkins in January on a tree opposite the Shirley Park Golf Club on the Addiscombe Road in Croydon

Right centre: A fallen leaf, more deeply serrated than native hazel, Prebend Gardens, Stamford Brook

Right bottom: Nuts litter the road, Sloane Street, Knightsbridge

Far right: A fine conical tree in late autumn, Howbury Road, Nunhead

THE THORNS

Crataegus spp. ✿ ✿ ✿ ✿ ✩

There are many hundreds of hawthorn, or simply 'thorn', species from Europe, western Asia and North America. Several of these small flowering trees are represented on our streets. They are often difficult to tell apart and, even when you think you have identified one, the experts can disagree on the exact species.

The most frequent Hawthorn encountered in London is the deep-pink-flowered **'Paul's Scarlet'**, which is described on the following pages. Inevitably, though, there are several more; here are a few of them.

Hybrid Cockspur Thorn (*C. x lavalleei*) is perhaps the other thorn most likely to be seen. It is a handsome hybrid, with large berries, more orange than red, persisting into the winter. Leaves are fairly smooth, but do have residual lobes. Unlike the true super-spikey **Cockspur Thorn** (*C. crus-galli*), a rather rare tree, this tree has a fraction of the spines of its namesake. At one time a popular choice, but less planted now, it makes a good avenue or specimen tree.

The **Frosted Thorn** (*C. prunifolia* **'Splendens'**) is similar to the Broad-leaved Cockspur Thorn, but more upright, with narrower leaves.

The thorn that appears to be in vogue now is the **Broad-leaved Cockspur Thorn** (*C. persimilis* **'Prunifolia'**) – like most trees of this genus, another product of the horticultural industry rather than a species that might be found in the wild. It is rather lovely: flowers and berries appear in bunches, and glossy oval leaves, larger than those of other thorns, turn a good range of autumn colours.

A tree that is a true species is **Scarlet Haw** (*C. pedicellata*), but it is rare. It has large red berries and lobed leaves similar to some Sorbus species.

Above: Hybrid Cockspur Thorn, Wandsworth

Right above: A young Broad-leaved Cockspur Thorn on the confusingly named Elm Grove in Crouch End

Right below: Bee-friendly flowers and glossy leaves of a Frosted Thorn

Far right below: Newly emerging leaves of Hybrid Cockspur Thorn, Eastbury Grove, Chiswick

PAUL'S SCARLET HAWTHORN

Crataegus laevigata 'Paul's Scarlet' 🍁🍁🍁🍁☆

The old-fashioned tree – seen all over including Peckham, Brixton, Clapham and Crouch End.

Sadly now out of favour, native hawthorns and their cultivars are rarely planted these days, so most specimens are elderly and may not be replaced.

There are two native spacies: *C. monogyna*, known simply as Hawthorn, which is common on open ground and in hedges, and *C. laevigata*, or Midland Hawthorn, found in ancient woodland. They are not easy to tell apart, can interbreed, and have several distinct cultivars with white, pink or red flowers, which bloom profusely after other flowering trees have finished, keeping the spring going well into May.

For this they were much prized in the post-war years, but their habit of leaning markedly appears to be the main reason they are much less frequently planted nowadays. It would still be great to see a London Hawthorn revival.

Paul's Scarlet (*C. laevigata* **'Paul's Scarlet'**) is by far the most frequent. It is a cultivar of Midland Hawthorn, and is also referred to as **'Double Crimson'**. As this name suggests, it has deep pinky-red flowers which are 'double', meaning they have two rows of petals.

In general, double flowers are less appealing to pollinating insects, but that doesn't seem to stop this tree producing a reasonable crop of haws in the autumn, a useful winter food for many birds.

Very similar to Paul's Scarlet is another cultivar of Midland Hawthorn, **'Plena'**, with double white rather than pink flowers. Never as popular as Paul's Scarlet, and seemingly completely out of fashion, this is now a rarity. I do hope it comes back into fashion: its white flowers are, I think, so much nicer.

A FASTIGIATE HAWTHORN

'Stricta' is a not infrequent fastigiate (with upward sweeping branches) cultivar of Common Hawthorn (*C. monogyna*). Good for a tight spot, perhaps, but it still has that leaning trunk! This one is on Edison Road, Crouch End.

Right: Newly emerged double flowers on a tree on a Rye Lane, Peckham tree

Far right: A handsome and large mature tree on Florence Road, Stroud Green

HOW MUCH IS A LONDON STREET TREE WORTH?

Chances are you value the trees on your street. Quite right, too. But have you ever thought of putting a price on that big old Plane tree, or that pretty little cherry?

You may be surprised to know that every street tree has a financial value ascribed to it. It's nothing to do with how much the timber is worth – this is an urban forest, not an upland conifer plantation or an ancient, traditionally-managed coppice woodland.

Rather, street trees are valued as community assets, and the monetary valuation (fortunately not as a tradeable asset) is to help those responsible for urban trees calibrate, for our financially-obsessed world, the benefits a tree provides, in terms of what would be lost should it disappear.

For example, street trees alter the character of neighbourhoods in a way that inevitably affects property values. A house on a street lined with century-old Plane trees is probably worth more than a house on a treeless street – but what part do trees play in that value?

Well, it could be argued that residents on leafy streets benefit from healthier lives because the trees are there: they soak up air pollution, dampen noise and regulate temperatures. But they also make the place look sylvan and picturesque. So tree-lined streets become more desirable, demand increases, and prices soon follow.

London is constantly in flux because of

redevelopment, growth, renewal and improvement; as a result, huge pressure is placed on our environment. Inevitably, trees may get in the way of progress – and this is where those values come into their own.

Imagine a new office development is planned, but some street trees are in the way. Planning permission would now require a compensation payment to the local borough for their removal.

An avenue of a dozen towering Victorian Planes could easily start at at £100,000 each. Presented with a potential bill of this order, the developers may well re-think their plans. If the trees really do need to go, then that compensation might be used to mitigate their demise by investing in new trees.

A street tree in London is valued using CAVAT, or the Capital Asset Value for Amenity Trees, a method devised by the London Tree Officers Association and now used by urban forest managers throughout the city. It's been so useful, in fact, that CAVAT has been adopted elsewhere too. Those fighting to protect the trees in Sheffield (see page 64) used it to draw attention to the value of trees targeted for removal there.

Essentially, the CAVAT framework uses three metrics. (There are many nuances, and a complex assessment would be needed for a truly accurate valuation). An initial valuation is based on girth: the bigger the tree, the bigger the bounty.

This is adjusted on a sliding scale, taking into account how much longer the tree might live: less than five years and the value is lost; more than 80 years and it stays at 100%. A little 'lollipop' cherry or rowan sapling, therefore, would hardly trouble the scorers.

Values are also adjusted for the density of population where the tree grows – more than 119 people per ha^2, and it goes up by 250%. In London, five inner boroughs have a density greater than this, with Islington top of the league at 151/ha^2. By this reckoning, a large Plane tree could be worth a staggering £466,990!

Left: Northumberland Avenue in the West End is lined with mature Plane trees, each worth at least £100,000

Above: A newly planted rowan like this one in Archway, on the other hand, might be worth little more than it cost to buy in the first place

HANDKERCHIEF OR DOVE TREE

Davidia involucrata

The glamour tree. Found in Chelsea, Highgate, Stoke Newington and Shoreditch.

'Wow!' Is what any rational person would exclaim when they first see a Handkerchief Tree in full flower, and with good reason: they are an astonishing sight. Flowering throughout May, trees are festooned with large dangling 'handkerchiefs', green at first, slowly turning dazzling white.

I was astonished to come across a few newly staked young trees in the boroughs of Kensington and Chelsea, Hackney and Islington. So far only a very few flowers have appeared, maybe because the trees are small and just getting used to their surroundings. It'll be fascinating to see how they develop and flower, but so far they appear to be coping well on the frontline.

Handkerchief Trees were discovered in China in 1869 by the French missionary and naturalist Père David, now commemorated in the tree's Latin name (*Davidia*). He also gave his name to an eponymous maple, another rare London street tree, and a species of deer. The first Handkerchief Trees arrived in Europe in the early 20th century, and the species has since gradually been taken into cultivation. The London examples are, as far as I know, the first to be planted as street trees, perhaps anywhere.

Notoriously difficult to cultivate, each Handkerchief Tree has to be grown from seed. Consequently, these trees are rare, not to mention expensive. The good news is, if they reach the age of seven, they usually prosper. I'm hopeful these pioneers will thrive and we'll see more planted.

A whole street of Handkerchief Trees is something I would travel to see in May. If I'm honest, I'd make the trip even in February.

Above: A shapely tree on New Inn Yard, Shoreditch

Right above: A Handkerchief tree in bloom, the flowers open a yellowish-green and mature to bright white within a few days. This one is in Kynaston Gardens, just off Stoke Newington High Street

Right below: Fruit on a Chelsea tree, Wilbraham Place

Far right below: A distinctive leaf on a Dresden Road, Highgate tree

BRAGANIA or ERECT CRAB APPLE

Eriolobus trilobatus, formerly Malus trilobata 🍁🍁✩✩✩

A refugee from troubled lands. Found in Hackney, Chelsea, Barnet and Gospel Oak.

Most of the names for this unusual small tree involve apple. Lebanese Wild Apple, Erect Crab Apple, Three-Lobed Apple... But though the fruit is said to be sweet and tasty – something to look out for in October, when it ripens to a yellow-green – it doesn't look that much like an apple to me.

Its botanical identity appears to be controversial even among tree boffins. Horticulturalists know it as *Malus trilobata* (an apple); a Greek academic paper, however, traces a taxonomic history that saw it previously classified as a hawthorn, a pear, even as a Service Tree. So it seems appropriate that its new scientific name is *Eriolobus trilobatus*: its own genus. I suggest we call it by its Greek name: 'Bragania'.

As well as the vagaries of botany, Bragania is a tree that reflects the politics of disputed lands. Its rarity in the wild, and a range that crosses the shifting sands of national and religious borders, has translated into the confusion of names in English.

It hails from the Levant, Anatolia and Thrace, and an arc of mountainous territory from northern Israel through Lebanon, Syria, western Turkey that ends in a few isolated European pockets in Greece, and Bulgaria. It is found at altitudes of 1,000 metres on Mount Lebanon, also home to the magnificent Cedar of Lebanon (*Cedrus libani*), a remnant forest which the Lebanese claim to be the last protected forest community of *Eriolobus*.

Further south, the tree is found in Israel's Upper Galilee, and on the slopes of Mount Hermon in the Golan Heights. In the Evros Mountains of Greece, Bragania trees have traditionally been safeguarded by local communities who value their fruit. When the pressure on land and resources in such regions becomes too much, however, the tree may be forced out.

Now Bragania has arrived in the capital as a welcome migrant, adding richness to the capital's increasingly diverse urban forest. Such an attractive tree: I hope it will be safe on London's streets.

Above: A Stoke Newington tree in flower

Right above: Large pure white flowers on a High Street, Barnet tree in May

Right below: Ripening fruits on a Dynevor Road, Stoke Newington tree

Far right: A typical upright tree on Dresden Road, Highgate showing good autumn colour

BEECH

Fagus sylvatica 🍁🍁☆☆☆

The elephant tree with a silver trunk. Found in Belsize Park, Denmark Hill and the City.

If Yves Klein's International Blue is the quintessence of blue, so the vivid green of fresh Beech leaves must be the truest expression of green. In mid-April, brown leaf buds swell and turn russet-orange, and then the first fissures of brilliant green start to unfurl.

I grew up with a huge Beech tree at the bottom of my garden. It was the first tree I got to know and love, so I may be slightly biased when I say it surprises me there are so few Beech street trees in London.

According to one urban forester, Beech presents several problems: its exposed roots push up pavements, and the root plate is often very shallow, so in storms Beech trees can topple more easily. But perhaps the biggest problem is the amount of nuts, or mast, they produce.

Although relished by squirrels and wood pigeons, Beech nuts are enclosed in inedible woody nut casings or cupules; in a mast year (when nuts are produced super-abundantly every three or four years), these discarded husks are deemed hazardous when crunched under foot.

This aversion to tree mess which informs many planting decisions may be justified on Oxford Street, but surely it's a small price to pay in residential streets, where big, native, architectural trees can add so much to a neighbourhood? Is it time we reappraised Beech trees?

There are several Beech cultivars, but perhaps the most promising for roadside planting is the fastigiate **'Dawyck'** form. It seems ideally suited for life on the frontline: slow-growing, neatly conical and ultimately quite small.

COPPER BEECH – THE FINEST PURPLE-LEAVED TREE?

Officially known as **'Purpurea'**, Copper Beech is surely the finest purple-leaved tree (a colour generally not suited to street trees, I feel). This one is on Longland Drive, Totteridge.

Right: The finest Beech-tree-lined street I know in London: Herne Hill Road off Denmark Hill

London has had its famous red double-deck buses for over a hundred years, and it has had trees on its streets – not least towering London Planes – for even longer. So how do you prevent the grand, outstretched bough of a mature London Plane in full foliage from doing a lot of damage to the top deck of a London bus (and, of course, any unfortunate upstairs passengers), or, at the very least, obscuring important road signs?

These days pruning street trees is easy: a couple of securely roped-up tree surgeons climb the tree, perhaps with the benefit of a cherry-picker, and the protruding bough is sliced off in seconds for the safety of all those aboard the number 11.

But before the days of abseiling and chainsaws, London Transport, as it was until 2000, had to go about the problem another way. Before 1986 it was also still responsible for all the green London Country buses that plied routes out into bosky Green Belt destinations like Rickmansworth and Dorking.

So, as you'll see from the picture above, London Transport seems to have had an actual Tree Pruning Department, which was equipped with a small fleet of customised vehicles. These were old service buses, chopped down from double-deckers of wartime vintage to open-toppers.

On the empty top deck of one of these treeloppers, secateurs in hand, would stand a London Transport official, attired, judging from the 1930s picture opposite, not in an old boiler suit with protective goggles, but in full serge uniform and peaked cap, to trim off the offending branches. Let's assume for his sake the bus was expected to come to a halt first.

Left: Formerly red London Transport bus number STL 1470, that saw service between 1936 and 1953, this vehicle was converted to open top as Tree Pruning Equipment, and is seen here in Regent Street in 2014 at a preserved buses rally, with its top-deck occupants wielding cameras rather than pruning shears

Above: Contemporary arboriculturalists pollarding a Plane tree on Hanley Road, Finsbury Park

Right: 31 July 1935, in the days before chainsaws and abseiling, a London Transport bus inspector carries out some delicate pruning of a street tree from the top deck of one of its treelopping fleet

THE ASHES

Fraxinus spp. 🍁🍁🍁☆☆

The ashes are difficult to tell one from another. Most are big trees with similar pinnate leaves (multiple small leaflets on a single stem), and all look very similar to our familiar native Ash tree (*F. excelsior*).

Apart from the Raywood Ash, described on the following pages, ashes tend to be only occasional street trees. The **Common Ash** (*F. excelsior*) is most often represented by a pair of cultivars. The first is the often overlooked **One-leaved Ash** (*F. excelsior* 'Diversifolia'), a tree that leaves many observers stumped as to its identity. It is large and familiar-looking, but the smallish, single, toothed leaves are quite unexpected. It appears to be a tree developed by a slightly wicked horticulturalist for no other reason than to confuse. For some reason, it is particularly common in the borough of Camden.

The other cultivar you may encounter is **Golden Ash** (*F. excelsior* 'Jaspidea'). It has good autumn colour and winter interest in the form of yellow-coloured young branches. It is often one of the first trees to turn: its golden autumn foliage can be spectacular.

Another ash that is best in autunm is the North American **Green Ash** (*F. pennsylvanica*). It takes on a fine golden hue slightly later than Golden Ash. Otherwise it is not dissimilar to other ashes, but has a slightly denser crown and more pointed leaflets that the native species.

Manna Ash (*F. ornus*) is a smaller, neatly rounded tree with smooth grey bark. Younger ash trees tend to be this species. What it lacks in size, it makes up for in attractive white feathery flowers, produced in May, and a fine autumnal display from October.

Sadly, all the ash species are no longer part of the planting palette due to the threat of Ash Dieback.

ASH TREES UNDER ATTACK

Ash trees are vulnerable to *Chalara fraxinea* or Ash Dieback, a fungal infection that kills trees. Sadly, the native Ash is especially susceptible, and it is expected that in the coming years the majority of trees will succumb. Street trees may be more resilient because of their relative isolation, while some species are less prone than others – the Manna Ash, for instance. But over the horizon in North America, ash trees of all species are being decimated by Emerald Ash Borer Beetle, a pest that hasn't arrived in Europe yet. But if it does, it could be disastrous.

Left: The confusing foliage of One-leaved Ash, Bernard Street, near Russell Square Tube station

Above: An autumnal Green Ash on Brookdale Road, Walthamstow, a street lined entirely with this species

Right: A Manna Ash in full flower during May, Ormond Road, Crouch Hill

RAYWOOD ASH

Fraxinus angustifolia 'Raywood' 🍁🍁🍁

A beautiful feathery tree, found throughout town from Bromley to Tottenham.

Almost too good to be true, Raywood Ash is a tree that looks great through the seasons, and can happily deal with all the usual privations of street-tree service.

However, its history is a cautionary tale. As they age, Raywoods tend to unexpectedly split apart, while re-growth from pollarding is ungainly, and rarely sprouts from the point of cutting. Consequently, they are gradually being replaced with other trees. Still, chances are the large ash tree on a street near you is a Raywood: from the 1970s to the 1990s this was a popular tree.

It is actually a cultivar of Caucasian Narrow-Leaved Ash, a species that ranges from Western Asia through to Central Europe. The **'Raywood'** cultivar itself originates from Australia. Specimens of a cultivar are cloned by grafting from a single parent tree – look carefully and you'll see a line near the bottom of the trunk where the original graft took place back in the nursery.

Grafting ensures consistency, but also means the bad characteristics are kept as well as the good. In the Raywood Ash, those bad characteristics did not become apparent until the tree had started to mature, by which time it had effectively gone viral.

In leaf the tree is stunning, its feathery foliage slinking in the breeze to form a mass of interesting shapes, while producing a single coherent crown. Throughout summer the leaves are a deep, fresh green, but it's autumn that sees the Raywood, or Claret Ash, come into its own. In a top-down flush, colours start to pop: the canopy dazzles with purples, magentas and golds.

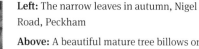

Left: The narrow leaves in autumn, Nigel Road, Peckham

Above: A beautiful mature tree billows on Wilberforce Road, Finsbury Park

Right: A tree in all its autumnal glory, Leyspring Road, Leytonstone

GINKGO

Ginkgo biloba 🍁 🍁 🍁 ✩ ✩

The great survivor. Found in East Dulwich, Earls Court, Victoria and Soho.

One urban forester described the Ginkgo to me as 'bullet-proof'. It has no known pests or diseases, and pollution just washes over it. This tenacity has built up over millennia – Ginkgos are ancient, and have been around for about 270 million years; they witnessed the demise of the dinosaurs. More recently, trees planted in Hiroshima survived the atomic bomb in 1945. So London's streets must be a walk in the park.

Being so ancient, Ginkgos are also primitive, and quite unlike any other tree. In the past they have been lumped in with the conifers, to which they do bear some resemblance, in shape at least. But their deciduous leaves ensured they left this camp, and they are now in a botanical division of their own, the *Ginkgophyta*.

Most street trees are male, which is bad news if you suffer from pollen allergies – male Ginkgo flowers produce a lot, and research suggests it is highly allergenic.

Female trees, however can produce large numbers of seeds, surrounded by a juicy outer skin – technically not a fruit – which has a particularly unpleasant smell (likened to rancid butter or even vomit), and can cause dermatitis if handled in quantity. Treated correctly, however, the seeds are edible, and are even a prized ingredient in some Asian dishes.

In China, Japan and Korea, Ginkgos have been in cultivation forever and are traditionally planted near temples, where they can reach great ages. Given their resilience to almost everything a city can throw at them, I predict London will be home to some amazing Ginkgos by about 3020.

DOES BOTANICAL SEXISM STALK LONDON'S STREETS?

For allergy sufferers, Ginkgos can be, literally, eye-watering. There are good, aromatic, reasons why urban foresters almost exclusively plant male Gingkos, but the consequences of this deliberate sexism are that there are now many, many more males around town than there are fruit-bearing females. Come the spring, and these hapess males just can't help themselves: from their rather small and inconspicuous flowers, they indiscriminately spew vast clouds of their male-tree-stuff in all directions. Tiny pollen particles drift around unseen, hopefully seeking out female flowers to fertilise, which will ultimately become those notoriously smelly ginkgo fruits. But because the ratio of male to females must be in the region of 10:1, those noxious gametes, with no receptive females to soak them up, instead get right up people's noses.

Left: The Ginkgo's distinctive bi-lobed leaves inform its botanical name, seen here on a Batavia Road, New Cross tree

Above: The notoriously smelly fruit borne on a rarely planted female tree outside the Royal Horticultural Halls, Greycoat Lane, Victoria

Right: A golden-foliaged tree on Turney Road, Dulwich in November

HONEY LOCUST

Gleditsia tricanthos 🍁🍁☆☆☆

The tree that could have your eye out. Found in Angel, Lewisham, Waterloo and Covent Garden.

For a tree with such a sweet name, Honey Locust has a fearsome side. It has the largest thorns of any street tree.

Most examples on our London streets, however, are thornless, of either the **'Inermis'** or **'Sunburst'** cultivars. The honey bit is to do with the seed pods: apparently the pulp contained within them is sweet-tasting, but should be left to the squirrels, as the pods can easily be confused with those of False Acacia, which has comparable leaves and smaller, but similar – and poisonous – seed pods. Those pods can be quite a sight (as well as a useful aid to identification), as they will cling on to some trees through the winter. They are large, anything up to 60cm long, wavy and an attractive deep reddish-brown colour.

Now, back to the thorns. They can also grow huge, up to 30 cm long, and they branch, for maximum security. With age, they become brittle and can break off, but the impression they give is of a tree not to be messed with. Trees sporting weapon-grade spines can be found on some very busy streets, including Upper Street opposite Islington Town Hall, where the danger posed to unaware passers-by could be considerable. Fortunately, local authorities will be well aware of the need for public safety, and regularly remove thorns up to eye height and beyond.

Otherwise, Honey Locust is actually a rather lovely tree. It is particularly good in tight spots, where it can fill space well and create a lofty, open canopy. It has the added advantage of rapid growth, allowing it to become a mature tree of considerable size. The tree's airy characteristic provides a very pleasant dappled shade and, especially where several trees have been planted, the effect can be memorable.

Endell Street in Covent Garden is a great advertisement for Honey Locusts: the raised canopy created by trees lining both sides of the road offers welcome shade to pub- and restaurant-goers spilling out onto the pavements.

Beware of Honey Locusts, though, they are spined!

A GOLDEN HONEY LOCUST

'Sunburst' is the cultivar currently in fashion: fresh yellow foliage emerges in spring, deepening to green as the summer mellows, and turning a splendid gold in the autumn. This one is on the corner of Elizabeth Street and Chester Square in Belgravia.

Right above: Seedpods and autumn foliage on a tree outside Lewisham Hospital

Right below: Thorns high up on a tree on Endell Street, Covent Garden

Far right: A mature tree on Stanley Crescent, Notting Hill

HIBISCUS

Hibiscus syriacus 🍁☆☆☆☆

A new glamour tree found in Shadwell, Kingston, Dulwich, Crofton Park and Shoreditch

Hibiscus are small trees with big blooms, coming in a range of colours. They started to appear on London streets just a few years ago, and have been turning heads ever since. But only in the summer.

These are not the bright red Hibiscus of Hawaiian hair attire though; that species, *Hibiscus rosa-sinensis* or the China Rose, is restricted to the tropics, and even on the mildest streets of London's urban heat island it would struggle.

Our Hibiscus, sometimes known as Rose of Sharon, comes from more temperate parts of Asia, and although its Latin name, *syriacus*, suggests it has its origins in the Middle East, it is actually a native of south-east China.

When Hibiscus is not in flower, there's not much to say about it. It has vaguely maple-like, deciduous leaves that can be slightly yellowish around the veins, giving the overall impression of trees not in the best of health. This is compounded perhaps by their diminutive size – these are not pavement shaders.

But all this is forgiven when they do flower, which can be for most of the summer. Several cultivars are present, along with another similar ornamental species, *Hibiscus* **'Resi'**. When planted in mixed groups the overall effect can be stunning, and not unlike strolling through a rose garden with several colours vying for your attention.

Garden Walk in Shoreditch is one of the best places to see them. Here there are pink ones, white ones, some with bright red centres and mauve ones too. This busy cut-through off Great Eastern Street represents an ideal urban Hibiscus plantation.

Above: A newly planted tree on Beckwith Road, Dulwich

Right: Flower of a **'Woodbridge'** cultivar on Garden Walk, Shoreditch

Far right: A **'Red Heart'** Hibiscus, again on Garden Walk, provides just enough shade for a solitary smoker on a hot day in August.

PLEASE WATER STREET TREES IN HOT WEATHER!

Especially during the summer months, it really helps if you water street trees. You can even pour your washing-up water or bath water into their tree pits – they're not fussy. But please avoid any water containing bleach: this has the potential to do considerable harm.

WHO PLANTS LONDON'S STREET TREES?

Many Londoners, I'm sure, would love to plant trees on their street. You can't simply find a vacant tree pit and stick in a two-foot sapling from the garden centre, though. There are lots of things to take into account: not least, money.

London's 33 local authorities, along with TfL, have the final say on what trees get planted where. Each employs urban foresters, or tree officers, whose job it is to look after them.

Every tree officer I've met is passionate about what they do, and will do all they can to stick up for their trees. But most rarely get to actually put trees in the ground. Their remit extends not just to the streets but the borough's parks, and indeed private gardens, where trees may have grown too tall or an ill-advised patio extension severed a stabilising root. So, in most parts of London, planting – including digging the tree pit and installing a tree guard – is contracted out. We can only hope the checks and balances are in place to avoid any repeat of Sheffield (see page 64).

Street trees are the most expensive to plant. Young trees need several years in the nursery to grow large enough to stand a fighting chance against the privations and hazards of their new, and decidedly unnatural, environment. Consequently, a single tree can cost hundreds of pounds. Add in preparing the ground, however, and then maintenance – especially important for the first three years – and the bill can run into thousands.

Years of austerity mean local authorities have had to prioritise their expenditure: should ever scarcer funds go to tree-planting or social care? Consequently, street-tree-planting budgets come from various sources, among them CAVAT valuations (page 82), the Mayor or the Government, and charities.

But with the benefit to the environment of street trees increasingly obvious, ordinary Londoners are taking matters into their own hands, and the borough leading the way is Lewisham. Never a wealthy part of town, its streets have been relatively sparsely planted, but that is changing.

Just take the Overground to Brockley to see the difference one group is making. In the last five years Street Trees for Living has planted a thousand trees around the borough, including the Persian Silk Trees now turning heads just outside Brockley Station (page 39), and its dedicated team of volunteers helps to maintain and, crucially, water the trees.

Elsewhere in Lewisham, Deptford Folk have been doing their bit to green SE8, with 200 trees planted to

mark the 200th anniversary of the publication of John Evelyn's diaries. They're hoping to do the same for the 400th anniversary of his birth. With the local community's help, Lewisham is transforming itself into one of the leafier parts of London. Surely a model for the rest?

Flushed with the success of the first edition of this book, the publisher has been talking to Hackney's tree officer and decided to get in on the tree-planting act. Hitherto you'd have had to go to Seville to see one of these in the street, but soon (keep an eye on my blog, *thestreettree.com*) it should be no further than Shoreditch...

Far left: A new Street Trees for Living Hornbeam goes in on Aldworth Grove, Lewisham. The tree was sponsored by local company Regular Cleaning, whose staff volunteered to help Lewisham's contractor Street Tree Care with its planting

Left: A contractor's truck loaded with new street trees destined for planting in Leytonstone

Above: Islington tree officer, Greg Packman, carries out the annual inspection of a magnificent Caucasian Wingnut on Highbury Station Road

WILLOW-LEAVED SANDTHORN

Hippophae salicifolia 🍁🍁✩✩✩

An unlikely urban upstart, seen in Stepney, Bermondsey, Shepherd's Bush and Islington.

This unusual tree has been around for some time, a rare sight on our streets with just a few examples in Southwark and Tower Hamlets. But all of a sudden, it seems to have hit the arboreal big-time, and is being put into pavements right across town.

When I first discovered some lining Curlew Street just off Shad Thames near Tower Bridge, back in 2011, I couldn't work out what they were. It was late December, and these intriguing tall, narrow trees were in full leaf with a few small orange berries nestling among the foliage. I'd not seen anything like them before.

Revisiting in February, I realised they were in fact deciduous, and a bell rang: Sea Buckthorn (*Hippophae rhamnoides*)! Could they be a tree form of our native maritime bush, renowned for the super-food qualities of its orange berries? But these were definitely trees, not mere seaside shrubs forced into tree form, despite their proximity to the river.

A helpful urban forester put me out of my misery. They were *Hippophae salicifolia*, he explained, known, confusingly, in the trade as 'Sea Buckthorn'. Further research led me to discover this species is very infrequent. In fact, it's so rare, it doesn't have a common English name. *Hippophae salicifolia*, I discovered, originates from high Himalayan river valleys many hundreds of miles from the coast.

Therefore, it seems a useful function of this book is to propose a more appropriate English name, especially as it appears to be increasing around town. The '*salicifolia*' bit of its Latin name references the similarity of its leaves (*folia*) to those of willows (*salix*), and, given that its home is so far from the sea, I suggest we name it **Willow-leaved Sandthorn**.

One of the reasons Willow-leaved Sandthorn is being much planted now is because it thrives in poor soils. It's also able to cope with all the usual privations of life on the street, and appears to be capable of dealing with the warm, arid conditions of heavily built-up areas. A trick it learned on a Himalayan mountainside.

Above: One of the Curlew Street trees

Right: The orange berries and willow-like leaves of a Stepney tree

Far right: A newly planted tree on Aylmer Road, Shepherd's Bush

WHY DO SOME STREET TREES HAVE CAGES AND OTHERS JUST STAKES?

Different boroughs have different ways to protect newly planted trees. Some use mesh cages, while others simply use a couple of stakes. Where trees are planted also matters –the more the footfall, the more likely you'll see cages.

GOLDEN RAIN TREE

Koelreuteria paniculata 🍁🍁☖☖☖

The tree for all seasons. Increasing all over town from Osterley, Chiswick and Putney, to Chelsea, Southwark and Hackney.

Golden Rain Trees don't do anything by half.

It's hardly surprising then, that they're beginning to be more frequently planted. Quite right, too: they're a good urban tree able to cope with pollution and hard surfaces. The only thing that seems to dampen their exuberance is shade.

Starting with spring, swelling red leaf buds explode into delicate rose- and bronze-tinted foliage which – I don't think this is an exaggeration – can hold its own with cherry blossom. Once fully emerged, those leaves are quite unmistakeable: they are pinnate like those of Ash and others, but are far more deeply toothed, sometimes actually further dividing so they can appear almost bi-pinnate.

The leaf show alone is a good reason to plant this tree, but it doesn't stop there. Flowers appear, if somewhat fleetingly, in late July. It is these that give the tree its Golden Rain handle, appearing as a yellow dusting floating in the canopy. Loose bunches of small flowers can be spectacular in high summer when very few other trees are in bloom.

And if the leaves and flowers were not enough, fruits follow: prominent, papery, three-sided lanterns that turn deep orange in the autumn and will survive into the following season.

For reasons that elude me, Golden Rain trees are also known as Pride of India: odd, given that the species is a native of eastern China, Japan and Korea. Maybe they are planted in temperate parts of the subcontinent?

The tenuousness of this connection did not stop one well-meaning urban forester planting a pair of Golden Rain trees in the shadow of the Indian High Commission just off the Aldwych, next to a statue of Nehru. I wonder how long this shade-intolerant pair will last in such an unsuitably gloomy spot.

I can imagine a street-planting scheme where alternate white-flowering cherries and Golden Rain trees would make a splendid year-round spectacle.

A NEWLY ARRIVED GOLDEN RAIN TREE CULTIVAR

A fastigiate cultivar has arrived! It's rare, but sure to become more popular. It has particularly upright and densely packed branches, so will work well where space is an issue. I have not yet seen it in flower, so I can only hope it gives as good a show as the regular species. Seen on Aylmer Road, Shepherd's Bush.

Above top: Seed pods, D'Oyley Street, Chelsea

Above middle: Young leaves on Reckitt Road, Chiswick

Right: The landmark Osterley Tube station tree on the Great West Road

Yes, is the simple answer. But the reasons are rather more interesting.

Only twenty years ago Hackney had relatively few street trees compared to leafier – and wealthier – boroughs further west. Now it's so well planted it's hard to see where any more could be crammed in. A quiet transformation has taken place, and the streets of this East End borough are now akin to an urban arboretum.

In today's multi-ethnic Hackney, Almonds rub shoulders with rare birches, variegated Tulip trees have been planted next to flowering Dogwoods. On one single street I've seen an Antarctic Beech, a Mimosa, a Handkerchief Tree and a Wild Service Tree. There's even a row of Dawn Redwoods down the central reservation of Mare Street! It's bold, even visionary planting and it's already created a diverse and unlikely tree collection so varied it could put some botanical gardens and arboreta to shame.

You can tell the moment you cross the borough boundary. Take a bus from Bethnal Green Tube station north towards Hackney Central. All the way up Cambridge Heath Road, in the borough of Tower Hamlets, you'll see traditional, mature street planting: outside the Museum of Childhood and York Hall Planes and Limes, for instance...

But the moment you cross over the Regent's Canal and the road becomes Mare Street, you'll see smaller, newer trees, of everything but. Welcome to Hackney.

Similarly less well-planted boroughs – Lewisham and Newham, for instance – are following Hackney's example and trying to catch up.

Some boroughs, like Southwark, encompass the tree-planting decisions made in the older, smaller boroughs they swallowed up. As we have seen, Bermondsey is notable for the legacy of Ada Salter and her predilection for the Tree of Heaven.

Other variations are a legacy of the remarkable freedom enjoyed by individual tree officers in former years. Islington is full of unsusual fruit trees. You'll find rare apples and pears from Archway down to Clerkenwell. Why? Because, it seems, for many years the borough had a tree officer who liked them.

Nowadays, planting policy is more codified. Camden, a borough thick with street trees, albeit mostly older than those in Hackney, has a policy, in line with other boroughs, stipulating 'the right tree for the right site', to achieve species and age diversity, with a priority for native trees of value to wildlife. Southwark, by contrast, has a planting list of no fewer than 65 species. Westminster has an inexplicable soft spot for the Chanticleer Pear.

We may discover that some unusual species make great street trees. If so, it should be known that Hackney was where they were planted first. On the other hand, what happens when trees get older, and a Black Poplar towers over a Mimosa?

There's a risk that streets have so many different trees, all different sizes and shapes, as to lack coherence. It's great to see a Victorian terrace in Stoke Newington planted with a range of small flowering trees, but it's also great to see an avenue, be that of Golden Rain Trees, American Sweetgums or good old Limes or Planes.

Left: A ripening Persimmon (*Diospyros kaki*) makes for a very unexpected sight on Dynevor Road, just off Stoke Newington High Street

Right above: A Peruvian Pepper tree (*Schinus molle*), the source of pink peppercorns, on a Southwark street

Right below: A Sand Pear (*Pyrus pyrifolia*), also known as a Nashi Pear, a tree only ever seen in Islington

CRÊPE MYRTLE

Lagerstroemia indica

The elusive flowering typo tree. Found in Holloway, Stockwell, Finchley and at the Angel.

Appearing in most of the literature as Crape Myrtle, this should surely be Crêpe Myrtle, as the tree is named for its showy, crimped, paper-like flowers. There are cultivars with deep-pink, magenta, mauve and creamy-white flowers to be seen. However these flowers are not guaranteed to appear in any profusion on our street trees.

Fortunately, this species is not just about the elusive flowers. In London the bark and the attractive, glossy foliage are where Crêpe Myrtles are really at.

Slim and shapely trunks are covered in one of the most pleasing barks of any street tree: smooth, light-grey to American tan in colour, it is naturally shed throughout the year, enabling trees to maintain clean, fresh colour.

A showy tree from east Asia, Crêpe Myrtle is commonly planted in Mediterranean countries, and also in California, where the late-season flowers bloom abundantly and predictably. It is a rare sight to see a London street tree put out much more than a shy bloom in early October, so it must be regarded as hopeful, or perhaps future-proof, planting here, as we wait for global warming to bring us up to the right levels of heat and sunshine.

Planting trees ready for a warmer climate may be a wise move: this tree used to be considered only half-hardy, but milder winters over the last decade mean that, sporadic flowering aside, trees in London appear to be thriving.

I admire this tree for blooming non-annually: it reminds us that ecological time has longer cycles than our own, and the surprise when it does flower is all the greater.

As yet, London's street-tree population is young. The trees illustated here are as big as they have got so far. It will be interesting to see how they mature, and if they prove a good long-term choice. Overall, it's an intriguing and beautiful small tree for a narrow, sunny street. We may, of course, be ready for Crêpe Myrtle sooner than we think.

Above: Crêpe-paper-like flowers on a Stockwell tree in late August

Right above: The attractive bark of a tree on Delhi Street, Barnsbury

Right centre: Autumn colour on a Percy Road, North Finchley tree

Far right: A rare sight: a tree in full bloom on Shaftesbury Road, Upper Holloway

HOW MUCH ARE ALL LONDON'S STREET TREES WORTH?

. . . .

Using the CAVAT system outlined on page 82, London's urban forest has been valued at a staggering £43.3 billion. This figure includes all the trees on our streets, in our parks, around our estates and in private gardens too.

CHINESE TREE PRIVET

Ligustrum lucidum 🍁🍁🍁☆☆

The bush that grew. Springing up all over town from Streatham to Harrow.

Tree Privet is related to the familiar hedging Privet (*Ligustrum ovalifolium*) of suburbia, but this is no mere bush: it is in fact a very fine, distinctive tree ideally suited to London's streets, where it prospers in almost every location.

Like its topiary-friendly cousin, Tree Privet appears to be ripe for the attentions of a creatively-minded pruner. I can imagine something very striking could be done with a whole avenue of closely spaced trees...

It is popular in a tight spot: planners and tree officers like it for roots that do not interfere with pipes or buildings, and for preserving a neat appearance with little maintenance. It's an evergreen species, so those glossy leaves continue to look good, and oxygenate their surroundings, throughout the year

In August and September Tree Privet becomes a bee magnet, as it flowers late and very well, with an intense heady scent. Apparently, though, Londoners do not universally love the aroma – but surely it is infinitely preferable to many other, more pungent urban bouquets?

Tree Privet is an example of a tree that was, until around 15 years ago, something of a rarity. But since then it has been planted extensively, and as it has done so well in a relatively short space of time, mature trees are now a common sight. This rapid population growth may have unforeseen consequences.

Experience from other countries suggests it could start to naturalise – definitely one to watch if our climate changes to become even more to its liking; only a few years ago berries were rarely produced, but in recent years, I have seen increasing numbers.

A STRIKING VARIEGATED TREE PRIVET

The variegated cultivar **'Excelsum Superbum'** can be very striking. Appearing yellow from a distance, it positively glows when in flower. Occasionally both this and regular Tree Privet are planted together; alternating avenue planting on a grander scale would certainly be worth trying. This one is on Elysium Street, Fulham.

Right above: Ripening small black berries, Stratton Street, Mayfair

Right below: Copious small and aromatic flowers on a Neal Street, Covent Garden tree

Far right: A fine-looking specimen in full bloom, Sussex Way, Upper Holloway

AMERICAN SWEETGUM

Liquidambar styraciflua 🍁🍁🍁🍁☆

The tree you could be forgiven for thinking is a maple is seen throughout London from Hounslow to Peckham.

American Sweetgums have been planted in almost every corner of London over the last 20 years or so, and the frenzy continues apace. Originating from the southern USA, Sweetgums are valued for their suitability for street-planting – even in our cool climate they take pretty much anything London can throw at them, and provide amazing autumnal colours too.

London needs big architectural trees, and as our Planes now have a range of pests and diseases lining up to attack, they are planted less frequently. This is where sweetgums come in: big trees able to reach 45 metres in the US. The tallest London Plane trees are huge, but still only around 40 metres. In the UK, though, sweetgums are unlikely to reach such great heights, and I am not sure they will ever have the character of Planes.

So named for the sweet, scented resin obtainable from crushing the leaves, sweetgums come into their own in October, when leaves start to turn a dazzling range of colours. The spectacle starts at the top of the tree and spreads down through the canopy well into December, and occasionally as late as January. It is one of the best autumn leaf shows of any large tree.

The leaves can easily be mistaken for maples or even planea, with their similar lobed, or palmate, shape. The easy way to distinguish a sweetgum from a maple is to look for globular flowers developing into seed balls; maples, on the other hand, flower briefly, developing characteristic winged seeds, or samara. Those balls though, may also be confused with Planes, in which case check the bark. Sweetgum bark is corky while Planes' is scaly.

Sweetgums are certainly beginning to make an impact on our streets. A whole avenue can be spectacular in autumn, Kelfield Gardens in North Kensington (see page 2), or Frankham Street in Deptford are excellent examples. I wonder what future generations will make of sweetgums? Might they come to be as loved as the iconic London Plane?

ANOTHER SWEETGUM

Chang's Sweetgum (*L. acalycina*), from Taiwan, is a very occasional London street tree. It has three-lobed, rather than five-lobed leaves. This example is on Half Moon Lane, Herne Hill.

Right top: Seed balls developing in autumn, Frankham Street, Deptford

Right centre: The unusual variegated form, **'Silver King'** seen outside the Emirates Stadium on Drayton Park

Right below: Typical corky bark on a mature Hammersmith tree

Far right: A glorious autumnal tree, Barforth Road, Nunhead

TULIP TREE

Liriodendron tulipifera

The big, handsome American hanging out in Dulwich Village, Olympia, New Cross and Belsize Park.

Is it the leaves or the flowers that give Tulip Trees their name? The striking leaves do, with a bit of imagination, form the silhouette of a tulip, perhaps. But if you thought that was the reason, you probably haven't spotted the remarkable flowers, which are a spit for those of the Dutch bulb.

Related to magnolias, the Tulip Tree produces abundant, large, cup-shaped flowers, but, unlike its cousins', these are far less showy. Only mature trees produce blooms, which can be hidden among the dense foliage and often high up in the canopy. Once found, however, the tulips are memorable: 5-8 cm across, with fresh green, yellow and orange parts, they are also much loved by bees.

If you find a tree with accessible flowers, it is well worth giving them a good sniff. They smell exactly like American cream soda!

Tulip Trees' tolerance of pollution and ability to get on in London have been known for at least two centuries, so it is surprising that there are relatively few large street trees here. An exception to this are the old trees lining Dulwich Village, which really show the potential for this species. But only now are we getting with the programme and starting to plant them more frequently.

In the second half of the 19th century, when street trees were being planted in a planned manner for the first time, the species those pioneer urban foresters chose were determined by what was easiest to propagate, transplant and establish: Plane, Poplar and Lime. Tulip Trees were less easy to handle.

Developments in horticulture mean propagation and transplanting are no longer an issue, but establishing Tulip Trees is slightly more tricky, and can take a few years. Once they are settled, however, they can last for 250 years and become as large as Planes.

A word of warning from America: as they mature, Tulip Trees have a tendency to drop branches. But if they prove suitable in the long run, Tulip Trees, with their blunt, oblong, even potentially iconic leaves, should give Planes a run for their money.

A NEAT TULIP TREE FOR A TIGHT SPOT

As with many trees, there is a useful fastigiate Tulip Tree. 'Fastigiata' looks good and fits the bill on busier, narrower streets where the regular species would be just too much. This one is thriving despite being on one of the most polluted corners of London – the A2, New Cross Road.

Above top: Distinctive blunt Tulip Tree leaves on Leonard Street, Shoreditch

Above: A large Tulip bloom hidden among the leaves on a tree on English Grounds, Southwark

Right: A youngish tree on the corner of King and George Streets, Richmond

THE MAGNOLIAS

Magnolia spp. 🍁🍁🍁🍁🍁

The trees that inspired paint manufacturers. Now found in Morden, Herne Hill, Chelsea and Bishopsgate.

Nothing gladdens the heart in early spring like a Magnolia in full bloom. There are a lot of different species and cultivars, and quite a few are finding their way onto our streets, which I applaud. Most have only been planted in the last few years, so we are still in an experimental phase, but whole streets planted with Magnolias could be magical places in early spring.

Magnolias are ancient plants that have been around since before bees (although not before Gingkos; see page 96), which may account for why their flowers are so large, evolving to offer protection against heavy, carapace-clad, pollinating beetles. The flowers are followed by cone- or candle-like, upright fruiting bodies containing individual bean-like seeds, sometimes quite colourful in their own right.

Familiar to many as a garden tree, **Saucer Magnolia** (*M. x soulangeana*) is the classic, usually multi-stemmed Magnolia of suburbia, flowering early in a variety of whites, creams and pinks depending on variety. I have yet to come across this species as a street tree.

Instead, described over the next pages are some of the trees that may be encountered on London's streets. Magnolia lovers would be well advised to visit Casino Avenue in Herne Hill, where Southwark's urban foresters have planted trees of the **'Galaxy'** cultivar to add an unusual feel to SE24.

Indeed, Southwark and Kensington and Chelsea appear to be leading the way with Magnolias, although at least one super-rare yellow-flowering **'Yellow Bird'** variety has been reported in Clapton.

Above: A **'Galaxy'** Magnolia brightening up a grey March day on Casino Avenue, Herne Hill

Right: The landmark group of slow-growing **'Merrill'** Magnolias in flower outside Borough Church

Between the flowers and the fruiting bodies, we have a lot of uninteresting leaves to look at which are nothing to write home about, and make identification rather tricky.

The exception to this is the most frequent and evergreen **Southern Magnolia** (*M. grandiflora*), originating from the southern US. Perhaps the least likely Magnolia, and therefore the easiest to spot, it has the biggest flowers of any street tree, which, unlike other Magnolias', open in July. Delicately scented, they will stay on the tree for some time, though not in great profusion.

Plenty of sun and warmth in a sheltered spot is required for this species to do well, so I was surprised to find a row in Bishopsgate opposite Liverpool Street Station. You'd expect them to prefer the wall of a stately home to languorously bloom against. Others can be found just off Tooley Street, on Magdalen Street in Southwark, outside Penhaligon's on the Kings Road, Chelsea, and outside Archway Tube station.

The Japanese **Kobushi Magnolia** (*M. kobus*) is another to look out for. One of the loveliest Magnolias, with starry white flowers of up to eight petals, it blooms in early March. It is small and very slow-growing. In Japan some venerable old specimens have become splendidly broad small trees. Considering that it arrived here 150 years ago and the first street trees started to appear only in the last 20 years, if this species can stick it we may be in for something special. An example can be seen on the corner of Langton Street and the King's Road in Chelsea.

Another March-flowering tree to look out for is *M. x loebneri* **'Merrill'**. Also a slow growing tree with Asian roots. A lovely group of these characterful **'Merrill'** trees can be experienced outside Borough Church, on the corner of Long Lane and Borough High Street.

Apart from the tropical-looking Southern Magnolia, it seems safe to assume other species will remain occasional, but beautiful centrepiece trees.

Far left: A newly planted Southern Magnolia in front of the Cheesegrater in the City

Left above: The Bishopsgate Southern Magnolias opposite Liverpool Street Station

Left below: A pristine white flower of a Southern Magnolia on Cadogan Gate, Chelsea

Above: Flowers of a **'Heaven Scen**t' Magnolia on Brunswick Place, opposite Bache's Street, Shoreditch

THE ORNAMENTAL APPLES

Malus spp. ✿✿✿✿✩

Trees that can give cherries a run for their money – found everywhere from Ruislip to St John's Wood.

There's more to the apple than the Cox, Bramley and Pink Lady, and a surprisingly diverse array of species and cultivars can be found on London's streets.

Street trees are about flowers, foliage and fruit, but not large, tasty, possibly dangerous or messy fruit. Ornamental apple trees have been planted for decades, so some old varieties can be seen alongside new urban upstarts.

Apples all have roughly similar leaves and flowers, although colour and size may vary. Apple bark is the key to identification: pretty much all trees develop scales or patches as they age, quite unlike smooth-barked cherries and rough pears.

Apples are less frequently planted than cherries, but in spring their blossom can be just as showy. Cherries get their fruiting over and done with in the leafy summer, but apples wait until the other end of the season.

An exception to the showy flowers rule comes in the form of the **Chonosuki Crab** (*M. tschonoskii*), which is perhaps the most frqeuent of the kerbside apples. You'd be forgiven for not having noticed it... This Japanese native is primarily planted for autumn colour and a much admired regular, conical shape, giving rise to its other name, Pillar Apple. Leaves turn to brilliant shades of yellow, orange, purple and scarlet, along with round, red-flushed, yellow-green fruits. When in flower (fleetingly), you might mistake it for a White-beam, as it has bunches of creamy flowers.

In contrast, one of the best flowering crab apples, *Malus* **'Evereste'** is also frequently planted. Pink-tinged buds open in April to reveal large white flowers,

HOW COME SOME TREES DON'T HAVE FULL BOTANICAL NAMES?

You may have noticed that, especially among the more ornamental genera, some street trees have short botanical names like *Malus* **'Evereste'**, or *Malus* **'John Downie'** – they seem to be missing the species bit. These names have been given to them by the horticultural industry. For instance, *Malus* **'Evereste'** was developed by the French agricultural research body, INRA, specifically as an ornamental flowering tree. It is the product of much interbreeding, and it is difficult to untangle its parentage in order to apply a species name, so, while they are cultivars, they are not cultivars of a specific tree you might find growing in the wild. It's the same for some cherries and magnolias.

Left: Pink and white spring blossom of a Japanese crab, (*M. floribunda*), on Greenway Close, Stoke Newington

Above top: Blossom on a '**Street Parade**' cultivar of Siberian Crab, *M. baccata*, on Kynaston Road, Stoke Newington

Above: Fruit of the '**Golden Hornet**' crab on Annette Road, Holloway

Right: An upright Chonosuki Crab with striking autumn colour, Marriott Road, Finsbury Park

developing into small orange fruit in the autumn. Combined with an even, conical appearance and love of pavements, this tree is spreading. '**Street Parade**' is similar but has pure white flowers.

There are several species of more old-fashioned crabs, often older trees that will no doubt be superseded by the neater, flashier trees now being developed. From the old school you might see the beautiful-in-flower but unkempt **Japanese Crab** (*M. floribunda*), or the characterfully twisted **Purple Crab** (*M. x purpurea*).

This species was much planted until the 1990s, but is rarely now, owing to a perceived untidy habit. As with other street trees, uniformity and ease of management are preferred. But one man's untidiness is another's character, and venerable specimens, with their arching trunks and unkempt canopies, have something of an old orchard about them. When in flower, Purple Crab can be quite a sight.

Similar but neater, deep-pink-flowering crab apples are now favoured: newly planted trees are likely to be either *M.* '**Profusion**' or *M.* '**Rudolph**'.

Some crabs have been developed for their fruit; of these, two are striking: '**Golden Hornet**' (*M. x zumi* '**Golden Horne**t') is renowned for clusters of golden yellow fruits staying on the tree well into the new year. They can be produced in such quantities that branches will bow under the weight. White flowers in April are also good. *M.* '**John Downie**' is another old timer noted for its fruit display. More traditionally apple-like, although smaller than eating varieties, it is edible and therefore a good fruit source for crab apple jelly.

With its historical penchant for fruit trees, Islington is a good place to seek out unusual apples, including a handful of **Yunnan Crabs** (*M. yunnanensis*) dotted around. Neighbouring Camden has had its own apple fervour, and I have seen *M.* '**Adirondack**', a nursery-produced North American with small leaves and white flowers here and nowhere else.

Left: A Purple Crab with characterful twisted trunk and stunning spring blossom on Forest Grove, Dalston

Above: Ripening fruit in late September on a specimen of '**John Downie**', Catford

WHY POLLARD THE STREET TREES?

You've almost certainly seen streets lined with neatly, even severely, pruned trees. It's particularly noticeable on avenues of Plane trees, which take on a distinctly sculptural quality after all the smaller branches have been removed. But it's not for aesthetic reasons that trees get chopped: it's much more practical than that.

Each borough is responsible for the trees on its patch, and has a responsibility to ensure the streets are safe and passable. That means making sure trees are healthy and there are no dead or weak branches that could fall on pedestrians, or low-hanging limbs that could hit buses and lorries.

But perhaps the most important reason why street trees are so heavily lopped – or pollarded – is to stop them getting too large. A large tree can be very thirsty, and a thirsty tree can quickly use up all the moisture in the soil. This in turn can lead to subsidence, which can be a very expensive business for local authorities.

If a crack develops in the wall of a house, the owner may try and sue the council, for allowing its trees to soak up all the water in the ground around the foundations. If the council can prove it pollards its trees every three years, then the courts will most likely reject the claim, on the basis that the trees have used up no more water than in previous years.

Picture: Recently pollarded Planes line Erlanger Road in New Cross

DAWN REDWOOD

Metasequoia glyptostroboides 🍁🍁🍁

The big deciduous conifer found all over, from the City and Canary Wharf to Bounds Green, Vauxhall, New Cross, Kensington and Ilford.

Just 5,000 endangered Dawn Redwoods survive in their natural habitat, a single Chinese forest near the city of Lichuan. These trees only became known to science in 1946, although the people who have lived with them for generations knew they were not like other trees, and named them 'Water Fir'.

Despite only making it to the West in 1948, Dawn Redwood has made it big. Its Latin name holds a clue to the heights this tree may attain: *meta* (like) *sequoia* (Giant Redwood, see page 176)... Unlike Giant Redwoods, though – indeed, the vast majority of coniferous trees – Dawn Redwoods are deciduous, which gives this tree a light, fresh appearance when in leaf, or, perhaps more properly, in needle.

Dawn Redwoods develop regular, conical shapes, but then so do many other conifers. So it's perhaps a surprise that such a rare and interesting tree has been the one favoured – over many other similarly architectural species – for the pavement. In this job it does very well, and has been widely planted, although, as its Chinese name suggests, it does like a drop of water, so young trees need to be properly cared for in order to establish themselves.

Urban tree planters have taken the Dawn Redwood to their hearts with some imaginative planting, often incorporating whole groves of trees. On the western edge of the City is an avenue of very tall trees behind the Royal Courts of Justice on Carey Street. Others surround the Gherkin. A traffic island spinney exists at the south side of Lambeth Bridge in Vauxhall. But perhaps the finest planting is further east: a whole forest glade, comprising dozens of trees, around Canary Wharf Tube station.

Dawn Redwood epitomises the experimental approach urban foresters take to the work of selecting and planting street trees. It is a tree that has been available for around 70 years, but has only been used as a street tree for the last 30, and yet we don't know how old – or how tall – it may become.

SIMILAR BUT DIFFERENT

There aren't too many deciduous conifers – most are evergreen trees like pines or spruces. But there is another tree that's very similar to Dawn Redwood, the **Swamp Cypress** (*Taxodium distichum*). It's a water-loving North American with subtle differences. It tends to be slightly less conical, and its needles are alternate; Dawn Redwood's are opposite. Seen on Junction Road, Archway.

Above: Foxy colouring of an autumnal
Dawn Redwood, here on Erebus Drive,
Thamesmead

Right: This sky-rocketing tree towers over
Onslow Square, Kensington

THE MULBERRIES

Morus spp.

Rare fruit trees: found in Lewisham, Hackney and Kennington.

Both the Black and White Mulberries put in very occasional appearances on London's streets.

White Mulberry (*M. alba*) is the most frequent in this role, although generally a much less common tree than its splendid sibling. In southern Europe, White Mulberries are a frequent sight by roads, particularly in rural locations. They are often pollarded and have whitewashed lower trunks – presumably to aid night-time drivers in steering a steady course.

London trees, however, do not share these managment practices and become venerable, spreading trees in only a few years. They are most remarkable for their foliage: a dense canopy of lush green leaves which can be different shapes on the same tree. Most leaves are large, elongated and heart-shaped (or cordate), while others can show an extra one or two lobes. Interestingly, older trees exhibit more lobed leaves than unlobed.

My favourite mulberry, though, is **Black Mulberry** (*M. nigra*), a tree I thought extremely unlikely to be encountered on a London street. I imagined I would have to be content with trees in old parks and squares, and occasional specimens overhanging streets, turning pavements purple in late August as their delicious fruits ripen and fall, uncollected.

I was thrilled, therefore, to be alerted to an old tree, a remnant of a Victorian school, rediscovered growing as a street tree on Pine Tree Way in Lewisham. And what a tree: old, twisted, and in late summer heaving with those delicious fruits!

White Mulberry trees give me goosebumps, but Black Mulberries are positively spine-tingling.

NOT A REAL MULBERRY

Paper Mulberry (*Brousonettia papyrifera*) is a street tree found in warmer parts of Dulwich, Peckham and Stoke Newington. Although loosely related to the mulberries, it is of a different genus, and its hairy fruit appear quite unpalatable. Instead, it is a tree historically used for making barkcloth – or paper – by Asian and Pacific island people. This one can be seen outside the Montpelier pub on Costa Street, Peckham.

Above: Lewisham's marooned Black Mulberry on the inexplicably named Pine Tree Way

Right: A newly planted White Mulberry on Walcot Square, Kennington

OLIVE

Olea europaea 🍁 🍁 ☆ ☆ ☆

The trendy tree found in Brixton, Pentonville, Paddington and Shoreditch (of course).

A remarkable choice for a street tree – wishful planting, perhaps – the attractive and long-lived Olive tree is not fully hardy here, but the examples planted in the last decade or so appear happy enough. I have never seen Olive trees lining city streets in Greece or Italy: is this peculiar to London? Maybe we northern European dwellers like them to remind us of warmer holiday destinations.

Small but nevertheless fruit-bearing urban Olive groves are to be found in several localities around town, where they blend in well. The silvery evergreen foliage mirrors the colour choices adorning the halls and doors of some homes in the more fashionable parts of London.

Olives are inedible until they have been through a complex process of curing and fermenting, so I am unable to report on the taste of London fruit. However, while regarding some Canonbury trees on a December afternoon, I witnessed a blackbird plucking a ripened olive from its branch, so they do have some takers.

Olives can be found in parts of Islington – indeed, the borough claims to have been the first to plant them on the street – reflecting its sizeable communities from several Mediterranean nations; and a nod, perhaps, to the glory days of the 1980s when media types consumed mountains of juicy olives to accompany the free-flowing Chardonnay.

The uses of the fruit of *O. europaea* are many and varied, as the ancients could testify: nowadays a locally sourced olive crop could supply London's burgeoning craft food industry...

Look out for Barnsbury Extra Virgin!

Above: A young Olive tree on Greenwich High Street outside the Picturehouse cinema

Right above: A small grove of aged but recently planted trees feature at the pedestrianised end of Canterbury Crescent outside Brixton Police Station

Right below: Ripening olives on Brooks Mews, Mayfair

SHOULD I PIN A LOST-CAT NOTICE TO A STREET TREE?

Sticking pins into street trees is a big no-no, not only because of the voodoo connotations of such an act, but also because puncturing the bark can be harmful. Pests and diseases can exploit wounds in trees to penetrate their inner workings. So, while street trees offer themselves as ready-made notice boards, it's best to tape your sign to an impervious metal lamp-post.

HOP HORNBEAM

Ostrya carpinifolia 🍁✿✿✿✿

An arboreal conundrum: found in Primrose Hill, Bounds Green and Hackney Wick.

Resembling, as its name suggests, the much more common European Hornbeam, this tree may easily be overlooked. Size, leaves and seeds are all similar, so those intent on a positive ID must look carefully. First of all, there are no fastigiate cultivars of Hop Hornbeam, so if your tree is wine-glass-shaped, it's a regular Hornbeam.

The main differences, then, are in the details. In spring Hop Hornbeam flowers appear as a fresh yellow hop – ovoid, and composed of multiple bracts (or scales), whereas Hornbeam flowers are catkins. As the seasons progress, Hop Hornbeam fruits retain the form of the flowers, becoming browner, and can stay on the tree after the leaves have been shed – another giveaway. Hornbeam flowers develop into hanging fruits with looser bracts, and by the time the leaves fall, fruits are unlikely to be seen. The bark of a mature Hop Hornbeam is also quite different: rugged and scaly instead of elegantly fluted.

All these similarities beg the question: if this tree is so similar to our beautiful, native Hornbeam, why is it planted at all? Apart from pandering to a small coterie of tree nerds, the answer is not obvious: given the option, I would go for Hornbeam every time. But there is another view...

One of the main concerns among urban foresters is developing resilience in the face of a growing number of pests and diseases threatening our trees. One way to lessen the impact of a devastating epidemic, like Dutch Elm Disease in the 1970s, is by building in species diversity: the greater the number of tree species, the less impact a pathogen affecting one species or even a whole genus might have on the cityscape.

A useful rule employed by many planters is '10, 20, 30': trees in a given area should not be more than 10% of one species, 20% of one genus, or 30% from a botanical family.

So this is one reason why the diverse, inclusive culture of our world city is reflected in our street trees.

Above: Flowers and leaves from one of a pair of trees next to Hogarth's statue on Chiswick High Road

Right: A mature tree across the road from the Pembroke Castle on Gloucester Avenue, Primrose Hill

PERSIAN IRONWOOD

Parrotia persica 🍁☆☆☆☆

The muscle tree: found in Peckham, Dalston, Primrose Hill and Beckenham.

Rare and lovely, with a tendency towards the gangly, Persian Iron-wood is a tree we are likely to see more of. Widely known as a large, multi-stemmed bush sometimes seen in parks, a single-stemmed cultivar named **'Vanessa'** – very much a tree – is starting to appear on our streets. Reports from the eastern USA have praised Persian Ironwood's toughness on the frontline, so in all likelihood it will do well in London too.

It comes into its own in the autumn when, in sunnier locations, its leaves turn a riotous array of hues, from purple through to orange, with an emphasis on reds. It appears shaded trees don't turn such magnificent colours, so it's one for the sunny side of the street.

At other times of year, this might be a tricky tree to spot, but it does have merit throughout the seasons. In winter, mature trees will produce bunches of – admittedly discreet – red flowers from January through to March.

These are followed by a dense canopy of blunt, oval leaves resembling those of Beech (see page 88), only slightly larger, but less papery, with what might be described as a 'waviness' to them. They retain a glossy green colour through to autumn, new leaves opening with a purple tinge.

It is the gangliness which I find most charming: new growth spurts out at unpredictable and ungainly angles, giving a chaotic overall appearance, suggesting this species might require more main-tenance in the future than other more foreseeably neat trees.

I'm a sucker for anything Persian, be it carpets, cuisine or trees, so the Persian Ironwood is of great interest to me. Originating from mountain forests near the Caspian Sea in northern Iran, there it mingles with other fascinating species also found on London streets, including the Caucasian Wingnut (page 164) and Persian Silk Tree (page 38). These unique forest habitats and the wild genepool they support are now endangered, so it would be sadly ironic if the future of this tree is confined to urban forests.

Above: Small red flowers appear in January, here in Peckham on the corner of Danby Street and Bellenden Road

Right above: Leaves and ripening fruits on a Primrose Hill tree

Right below: A Downham Road, Hag-gerston, tree

Far right: A typically gangly, and spec-tacularly coloured tree on Finsbury Park Road in early November

FOXGLOVE OR PRINCESS TREE

Paulownia tomentosa

The unpredictable showstopper that isn't a Jacaranda. Found in Deptford, Stoke Newington, Dulwich and Brixton.

Foxglove Trees are unreliably spectacular. One of a very few blue-flowered trees happy to grow in London, this is the only one likely to be found on the street. In a good year its flowers can be abundant, indeed, head-turning, but while this azure explosion happens most years, it's not something we can take for granted.

Flower buds start to develop in late summer, and have to steel themselves through the winter until the following May. Perhaps this is just too demanding, and once in a while the trees just need a rest, resulting in the occasional 'off' year.

Much more reliably, after flowering the leaves appear. Huge, they resemble those of the Indian Bean Tree (see page 62), but are slightly pointier, with five subtle but distinct lobes. Unlike that species' signature beans, Foxglove Trees bear seeds in oval capsules that stay on the tree through the winter alongside the developing flowers.

In China, from where this tree hails, it is tradi-tionally planted at the birth of a baby girl. By her marriage, the fast-growing Foxglove Tree will have attained a considerable size, and is cut down to pro-vide wood for carving decorative items for her dowry. This practice is where, apparently, it gets its 'Princess' name from. Personally, I much prefer the 'Foxglove' appellation, which offers a fair description of its trum-pet-like flowers if not their colour.

That same human timeframe may well fit into their average lifespan on a London street tree. Given their size, they may well be ready for removal after thirty years: let us hope the wood is put to good use.

IS IT OK TO PLANT UP THE TREE PITS ON MY STREET?

Yes! The practice of planting tree pits started as 'guerrilla gardening' – people planting up aban-doned, unloved or disused plots of land, but now it's gone mainstream... In some parts of town res-idents have planted around the trees along whole streets. Some boroughs even issue advice on what to plant and when. Streets with planted pits not only look good; they feel safer and more cared-for too. But a word of warning: only plant annuals or biannuals, or maybe a few bulbs; perennials, such as shrubs, may out-compete the tree.

Right: Tidemill Way in Deptford is a short street planted exclusively with Foxglove Trees. Visit in early May for the dramatic show

THE PINES

Pinus spp. 🍁🍁☆☆☆

Rare but increasing. Found on the streets of Camden, Dalston, North Greenwich, Kings Cross, Chingford, Chelsea and Vauxhall.

It may be surprising to learn that only a few years ago, the number of pine trees planted as street trees could probably be counted on the fingers of two hands. In fact, conifers generally, with the exception of the Dawn Redwood (see page 128), have been almost as rare as hen's teeth. But that is beginning to change.

So what are the reasons for this coniferphopia? Are pine needles seen as dangerous by overzealous Health and Safety types? Are they just too Christmassy, or do they not fit for some other reason? Vast coniferous monocultures carpeting Lake District hillsides or desecrating Scotland's Flow Country have certainly not done much for their reputation.

On the face of it, there are lots of good reasons to plant more coniferous trees: year-round pollution reduction; greater screening potential; and, of course, better year-round noise muffling. These 'ecosystem services' are things that all street trees provide, but during the winter, deciduous trees are not half as good at them as evergreens. Having more conifers would provide greater diversity, and therefore interest in the urban forest.

Having spoken to several urban foresters about this gap in the canopy, I've found the main reason appears to be merely fashion: they're not on the radar because there are no precedents, and it might seem potentially risky to plant something different from a Plane or cherry.

But that has not stopped interesting experimentation with other species: common street trees like American Sweetgums, Himalayan Birch and Juneberry were once exotic rarities.

Perhaps conifers are perceived as so radically different from other trees as to seem a step too far. I imagine the Dawn Redwood was able to sneak in on account of its deciduousness.

Gradually and quietly, though, experiments are going on. I have come across **Austrian Pine** (*P. nigra*), **Scots Pine** (*P. sylvestris*) and one or two **Stone Pines** (*P. pinea*), the source of pine nuts, that essential pesto ingredient. As pines are very difficult to identify, especially for a Londoner with a wealth of broadleaf trees to regard, I am tentatively going to say a lonesome **Monterey Pine** (*P. radiata*) grows in Chelsea too.

Other conifers are gradually appearing too: **Larches** (*Larix decidua*) in Hackney, **Giant Redwoods** (see page 164), and one or two cedars including North African **Atlas Cedar** (*Cedrus atlantica* **'Glauca'**) and Himalayan **Deodar** (*Cedrus deodara*), but as yet the wonderful **Cedar of Lebanon** (*C. libani*), have not been reported.

Hackney, inevitably, is a great place to see how pines might be used in the future. Newly planted in small groups on wide pavements and pedestrianised areas, they can provide year-round interest.

Right above: A group of Austrian Pines at the Elephant and Castle

Right below: A Scots Pine on the corner of Dalston Lane and Queensbridge Road, Dalston

Far right: The tentatively identified Monterey Pine just off the King's Road on Manresa Road in Chelsea

Just as you can go to Pimlico and, arboreally, suddenly find yourself in a corner of Australia, so, not far away in Vauxhall, is another antipodean oasis.

In the early 1980s Bonnington Square was squatted. The houses there had been compulsorily purchased, legal complications ensued, and they remained empty and dilapidated.

The new residents quickly set about making this broken and barren corner of London their home, and steadily transformed it into the green oasis it is today. Bonnington Square Gardens were created – a nod to the vanished and legendary Vauxhall Pleasure Gardens nearby – and over the years there has been extensive street planting.

New Zealand is the country of origin for many of the square's long-standing residents and, for some of the chosen street trees too. On Vauxhall Grove, leading into Bonnington Square from Harleyford Road, stands a **New Zealand Lacebark** (*Hoheria sexstylosa*), while palm-like **Cabbage Trees** (*Cordyline australis*) (see page 72), and the frankly bizarre **Lancewood** (*Pseudopanax crassifolius*), are dotted around.

Other highlights include a **Hybrid Strawberry Tree** (*Arbutus x andrachnoides*) (page 48), an **Italian Cypress** (*Cupressus sempervirens*), several unusual **Beech** (*Fagus sylvatica*) cultivars (page 88)and a **Stone Pine** (*Pinus pinea*). This list is by no means exhaustive: there are other interesting, if slightly less unusual, trees to see – the square is well worth a visit.

Bonnington Square is more like a garden than any other street I know in London. All the planting, and indeed the maintenance, is done by the residents, in a spirit of community born out of the original squatting culture. Such haphazard planting may not suit every location, but it offers a glimpse of a possible garden city, where trees, plants and urban environment all merge, beautifully, into one.

Left: The Italo café is shaded by a Judas Tree, while a Lancewood stands guard on the street corner

Above: The Italian Cypress and Stone Pine complement one another on the kerb

Right: Two fastigiate Dawyck Beeches, one the unusual purple-leaved form

LONDON PLANE

Platanus x hispanica, or P. x acerifolia 🍁 🍁 🍁 🍁 🍁

The tree that defines London. Towering London Plane trees can be seen in Westminster, Pimlico, Kennington and Holborn.

No book on London's street trees would be complete without the tree named after this great city: the London Plane. Towering, graceful trees line major thoroughfares, form leafy residential avenues, and provide height and structure to parks and gardens everywhere. They define the capital as much as black cabs and red buses.

It wasn't always so. The tree known the world over as the London Plane, and by Londoners simply as the Plane, only arrived on these shores in the late 17th century, from Spain or France. It is a hybrid of two transcontinental cousins: the **Oriental Plane** (*P. orientalis*), a tree of south-east Europe and western Asia, and the **Occidental Plane** (*P. occidentalis*) or American Sycamore, from the eastern USA.

Being a hybrid, the London Plane is more vigorous than either parent species and can attain great age and height. The two earliest known trees introduced to the UK are still alive and kicking – one, officially a Great Tree of London, grows in Barnes and is known, appropriately enough, as 'Barney'. (The other grows at Ely Cathedral.) It seems, then, that even the oldest street trees, at a mere 150 years old, probably have centuries left in them.

The first street trees planted systematically in London were Planes, and these pioneers from the mid-19th century can still be seen along the Embankment from Westminster to Blackfriars, some surviving originals now attaining elephantine proportions. Other early Plane avenues include streets around Westminster such as Northumberland Avenue.

Even more glorious early and original trees can be seen in South London forming a vaulted green tunnel along Kennington and Kennington Park Roads. These early plantings were so successful they started a craze for street trees, as civic-minded Victorians started laying out new streets all over the city.

Other, later examples of Plane planting can be seen on the Millbank Estate behind Tate Britain, Kingsway in Holborn and in the late-Victorian and early-Edwardian suburbia of Muswell Hill.

NEIL A.
ARMSTRONG

APOLLO MOONSHOT TOUCHES DOWN IN KENNINGTON

. . . .

Tree-conscious top-deck travellers on a 3, 59 or 159 bus sailing down Kennington Road will have noticed the fine London plane trees lining this leafy boulevard. But only the sharpest-eyed will have noticed the small metal tags attached to each tree on the western side of the street between the junction with Kennington Lane and the Imperial War Museum.

At the northern end, a tag bears the name 'Harrison H. Schmitt' and, just after the Texaco garage, 'Neil A. Amstrong' can be seen. In all there are 16 little metal plaques. There were once 24, representing every Apollo astronaut. The tags have been on the trees since at least 1990, maybe even longer, and, as well as some tags going missing, some of the trees have gone too. At least one succumbed to the arrival of a gas main, and another was removed after a 59 bus crashed into it in 2013.

So who put them there in the first place? There has been much speculation over the years, but a 2018 report in a local newspaper confirmed the British Interplanetary Society, based on nearby South Lambeth Road, was responsible.

London's Plane trees have survived industrial pollution from Victorian times, the devastation of the Blitz, pea-souper smog up until the 1960s, and ever-increasing vehicle exhaust fumes. Regularly flaking bark enables them to jettison built-up pollution and keeps trees looking fresh.

Planes in London are characterised as huge trees with massive open canopies; many street trees, however, are regularly pollarded to keep them to a regular, even shape and size. The species can deal with this quite happily, but it does limit the really towering, awe-inspiring impact un-pollarded trees can have on a street.

Where all the trees planted during the roughly 50 years between 1865 and 1915 came from is now lost in the mists of time, but there is clearly variation between them. Some have great unbranched trunks with smooth flaking bark, others much less smooth trunks and branches that appear lower. Others again exhibit burrs, while there are differences, too, in how incised the leaves are.

How come such variation? It seems there are different clones or cultivars around town, often quite local in their distribution, and probably unnoticed by planters at the time. Trees have been managed differently, too, which can affect where branches begin or how these limbs are shaped.

London without Planes: wouldn't it be like the ravens leaving the Tower?

Previous page: The Windrush Square Plane, Brixton

Left above: Newly planted Planes line the new Embankment in front of Somerset House, 1876

Far left below: Plane leaves frame Big Ben

Left below: Distinctive winter seed pom-poms hang from one of the Victoria Embankment trees in Westminster

ORIENTAL PLANE

Platanus orientalis 🍁🍁☆☆☆

Mum, or dad, to London Planes. Seen occasionally in Chelsea, Whitechapel, Kensington, Chiswick and Crouch End.

In an Oriental Plane you can see what gave birth, effectively, to London's truly iconic street tree – once upon a time there were none of them: only these, in... faraway Byzantium.

The Oriental Plane actually comes from Europe, not from east Asia as its name might suggest. When it acquired that Oriental bit, the Orient didn't mean much further than Athens or Istanbul. That was quite some time ago, of course, and this tree has been around for some time too. The great 17th-century dendrophile, diarist and Deptford resident John Evelyn had one growing in his garden, and in his book *Sylva, or A Discourse of Forest-Trees and the Propagation of Timber* of 1664, encouraged others to plant them too. He also recounts how the Romans would feed them with wine.

So Oriental Planes are pretty special trees, and they are also quite rare. For a tree that has been here for at least 350 years, the oldest in London is probably one at Kew that dates to the 1700s. It is only in the last few decades that urban foresters have started to plant them on London's streets.

As we know, Oriental Plane is one of the parents, along with the American Sycamore, of the hybrid London Plane. The American species does not thrive in our damp, cool climate, so is virtually unknown. Therefore you can narrow down your Plane identification dilemma to two species, one of which is half of the other one anyway.

How do Oriental Planes differ from London Planes, then? Well, telling them apart can be can be

quite tricky, as they are of similar size and shape and have similar bark. But Oriental Planes have more deeply incised leaves, and they also tend to have more seed balls. A London Plane will have two or three large round fruiting bodies on a dangling stem, while Orientals have up to seven, smaller balls. Oriental Planes have a markedly fresh aroma to their new leaves in spring too, an attractive feature they did not pass on to London Planes.

Of the Oriental Planes seen on the street, two cultivars that are likely to be encountered, among newer plantings at least. **'Digitata'** has very deeply incised leaves, giving the canopy a light feel, while **'Minaret'** is similar with only slightly less incised leaves.

Oriental Planes were part of the original planting scheme on the Victoria Embankment back in 1870, and one or two old trees lurk among the mostly London Planes. One of the trees on the corner of Horse Guards Avenue might have what it takes.

Right above: Distinctively incised leaves and smaller seedballs on a Pond Square, Highgate tree

Right below: A young **'Minaret'** cultivar on Frampton Park Road, Hackney

Far right: A row of **'Digitata'** cultivars outside Waterstones on the King's Road, Chelsea

WHAT DOES THE FUTURE HOLD FOR LONDON'S PLANES?

Our magnificent and symbolic London Plane trees, landmarks of London from Northumberland Avenue to Bethnal Green, Kennington to Harrow, are under threat on several fronts.

Wander through the urban forest in high summer and you may notice Plane trees with wilting leaves and young shoots. This is anthracnose, a fungal infection that varies in severity from year to year. While it is unsightly, at least it won't kill the tree.

Worse is massaria, another fungal infection that affects trees under stress from drought, causing leaves and branches to fall prematurely. This disease is manageable, by removing affected branches before the disease can really take hold, so vigilance is required to spot the symptoms.

The worst threat, though, is plane tree wilt, yet another fungus, imported accidentally into southern Europe from North America during the Second World War. This disease causes canker, or tree bleeding, wilting, and ultimately death. It has gradually spread north through Italy and Switzerland, and is now in France. Plane trees along the Canal du Midi in the south of the country have succumbed, and large numbers have been lost. With climate change it is expected this disease will only increase its range, and if it ever gets this far north it could be devastating to London.

Yet another potential problem facing Planes is drought. In their natural habitat, both parents of the London Plane grow along river beds, which often run-dry in the summer. The trees like moisture, but can cope with arid spells by opportunistically soaking up these residual streams when they are in spate. But, as massaria shows, drought stress can cause pathogens to take hold.

Plane trees on London's streets have done well in the past, it is thought, because the rainfall has been just right, but also because we have spongy clay soils from which Planes can extract moisture when rainfall runs straight off hard ground surfaces. Leaky Victorian water mains have helped by seeping moisture straight into the soil – perhaps for our Planes acting like a dry river bed.

But in recent years a major programme of reducing water leaks across London has seen 19th-century water pipes gradually being replaced by nice new blue plastic ones. So, goes one theory, this may exacerbate the drought stresses on our Planes, and make them yet more susceptible to disease.

With the prognosis for Plane trees so uncertain, some boroughs have stopped planting them. But others are still, favouring cultivars like '**Malburg**' which offer some resistance to the threats now posed.

Perhaps the best thing we can do is be vigilant about importing trees, get tougher with bio-security, and monitor all our Plane trees regularly. London's Plane tree heritage is unique: we should keep planting them. Enjoy these great trees while you can.

Left: The towering canopy of Kennington Park Road

Right above: A newly planted Plane tree takes centre stage in Wolfgang Suschitzky's beautiful 'Fog at Cambridge Circus', 1937

Right below: A newly planted Plane on Whitechapel Road, 2019

THE POPLARS

Populus spp. 🍁🍁☆☆☆

The big, billowy riverside tree. Found in Bethnal Green, Muswell Hill, Deptford, Barnes and Bermondsey.

The tree after which the East End district of Poplar is named is the very rare and stately native **Black Poplar** (*Populus nigra ssp. betulifolia*), king of all the poplars in London. In earlier times, before the Thames was embanked and anywhere remotely marshy drained, the damp alluvial soils of this estuarine hamlet represented the tree's ideal habitat.

Now only a few old Black Poplars survive, on the upper reaches of the river around Hammersmith and Barnes, where their enormous silhouettes form a familiar backdrop to the annual Oxford and Cambridge Boat Race.

Most poplars found on London streets these days are **Hybrid Black Poplars** (*P. x canadensis*) a cross between the European Black Poplar and the North American Eastern Cottonwood. Alongside London Plane and Lime, such poplars were popular with Victorian and Edwardian urban foresters, who planted them extensively, valuing uniformity and vigorous growth rates for newly developed suburban avenues.

One of the most impressive street trees if left to grow, Hybrid Black Poplar does not, however, appear to be long-lived, and is rarely planted now. Consequently it's quite uncommon, and represented by only a few large survivors: occasional, heavily pollarded avenue trees, remnant trees from former gardens and some magnificent riverside trees.

Other poplars are also present in London: **Aspen** (*P. tremula*) and **Grey Poplar** (*P. x canescens*) can occasionally be seen. Both are distinctive: Aspen's round, serrated leaves flutter in the slightest breeze, and Grey

Poplar has diamond-shaped marks on the bark of older trees.

As a street tree, the true native Black Poplar is unknown, but the familar fastigiate **'Italica'** cultivar of field edges is present. This is the '**Lombardy Poplar'**. It has been planted in the past, but I have not seen a street tree less than 20 years old.

Poplars are dioecious, meaning the male and female flowers are borne on separate trees. Planted trees tend to be male, so the remarkable sight of seed dispersal from female trees is relatively rare. In early summer, female poplars release plumes of seeds surrounded by cotton-like down, hence the common American name of '*Cottonwood*'.

Right: A Lombardy Poplar next to Tower Bridge on Shad Thames

Far right: Typical heavily pollarded Hybrid Black Poplar on Coppetts Road, Muswell Hill

THE FLOWERING CHERRIES

Prunus spp. 🌸🌸🌸🌸🌸

'Loveliest of trees the cherry now...' Found every-where from Acton to Walthamstow, and Chingford to Wimbledon.

Show me the person who doesn't love cherry blossom. Along with crocuses and daffodils, it is one of the quintessential harbingers of spring. London is well garlanded with a bewildering array of flowering cherries, blooming from November right through to May.

The genus *Prunus* does not limit itself to cherries: it also contains the plums, peaches, apricots and almonds. Our flowering street-tree population consists of species right across this range. Over the next couple of pages I highlight, roughly in order of their flowering, some of the more frequent or notable species. But to do justice to all London's *Prunus* species would require a book of its own.

Perhaps the most misunderstood species is the **Winter Flowering Cherry** (*P. x subhirtella* 'Autumnalis'), which gets going in November and doesn't stop until April. It can be a surprise to see this tree in full flower in the depths of December, but don't worry, it's not climate change!

Otherwise, some of the earliest trees to flower, and some of the most common, are the purple-leaved **Cherry Plums**, *P. cerasifera* 'Nigra' and 'Pissardii'. Flowering early – February is not unusual – they can have a good show of small, white or pink flowers respectively. However, for this fleeting early show we have to put up with the most deadening purple-leaved trees known to man the rest of the year.

Other early flowering types are pink-flowering *P.* 'Okame', and **Almond** (*P. dulcis*) with its large pink or white flowers. Look out for fluorescent pink-flowering **Hybrid Peaches** (*P. x amygdalo-persica*) in Hackney.

By March, cherries are beginning to get into their stride, and three species stand out: **'Accolade'**, with lovely pale pink flowers; the magnificent **Yoshino** (*P. x yedoensis*), a wonderful white-flowered cherry much valued in Japan, where it is the most frequently planted species in Tokyo; and **'Snow Goose'** or **'Umineko'**, is a distinctive goblet-shaped tree currently very popular with street planters.

As April gets going, so the cherries do too. Look out for our native **Wild Cherry** or **Gean** (*P. avium*), a big tree that can give most of the Japanese cultivars

Left: Flowers and emerging leaves of a **'Nigra'** Cherry Plum on Amersham Vale, Deptford

Above top: Almond blossom in January, Finsbury Park

Above: Frostbitten Winter Flowering Cherry blossom, Charles Street, Mayfair

Right: A neat, vase-shaped **'Snow Goose'** on Highbury Station Road

a run for their money. The double-flowered cultivar 'Plena' is often seen on the street.

Spire Cherry (*P. x hillieri* 'Spire') is also frequent and is relatively easy to identify by its long, tidy, upward-arching branches. *P. serrulata* 'Amanagawa' is a good cherry for a narrow street, as it maintains a neat fastigiate form. It also has attractive, single pinky-white flowers.

As April progresses some of the showiest species make themselves known. And they don't come much showier than 'Kanzan'. Big and blousy pink blooms characterise this, the classic cherry of suburbia. 'Pink Perfection' is similar, but with slightly paler flowers. Cecile Park in Crouch End is an excellent example of a Kanzan avenue. Competing with Kanzan in the gaudy stakes is a new arrival, 'Royal Burgundy', a species that would make the grandfather of British cherry-tree planting, Captain Collingwood Ingram, turn in his grave. It combines the worst features of Kanzan – overblown pink blossom – with the worst feature of a cherry plum: purple leaves.

The variety with which 'Cherry' Ingram is famously associated is an occasional street tree: the 'Great White' or 'Tai Haku', a long-lost Japanese tree with the largest of cherry flowers, which he rediscovered in a Sussex garden in 1932.

In May the last cherries flower, including the native Bird Cherry (*P. padus*), with spikes of white flowers, and the Manchurian Cherry (*P. maackii* 'Amber Beauty'), a species planted for its bronze bark rather than its inconspicuous flowers.

At one time cherry tree avenues with consistently-sized trees of the same species were popular but, while many older suburban avenues remain, this style, with the notable exception of Winterbrook Road in Dulwich, appears to be now out of fashion.

What a shame: whole streets of flowering trees look great, but avenues of most species can be magnificent. Wouldn't it be lovely to revive this practice?

Far left: Cecille Park, Crouch End, is a street planted exclusively with 'Kanzan' cherries

Left above: 'Royal Burgundy' on Gresley Road, Highgate

Left below: Bark of an 'Amber Beauty' Manchurian Cherry Wharfedale Road, Kings Cross

Above: A magnificent native Wild Cherry, Homefield Road, Chiswick

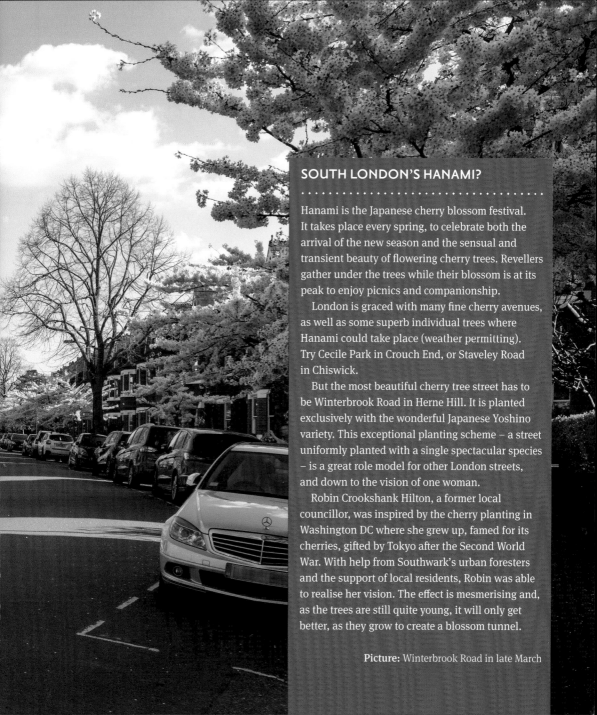

SOUTH LONDON'S HANAMI?

Hanami is the Japanese cherry blossom festival. It takes place every spring, to celebrate both the arrival of the new season and the sensual and transient beauty of flowering cherry trees. Revellers gather under the trees while their blossom is at its peak to enjoy picnics and companionship.

London is graced with many fine cherry avenues, as well as some superb individual trees where Hanami could take place (weather permitting). Try Cecile Park in Crouch End, or Staveley Road in Chiswick.

But the most beautiful cherry tree street has to be Winterbrook Road in Herne Hill. It is planted exclusively with the wonderful Japanese Yoshino variety. This exceptional planting scheme – a street uniformly planted with a single spectacular species – is a great role model for other London streets, and down to the vision of one woman.

Robin Crookshank Hilton, a former local councillor, was inspired by the cherry planting in Washington DC where she grew up, famed for its cherries, gifted by Tokyo after the Second World War. With help from Southwark's urban foresters and the support of local residents, Robin was able to realise her vision. The effect is mesmerising and, as the trees are still quite young, it will only get better, as they grow to create a blossom tunnel.

Picture: Winterbrook Road in late March

Trees often feature in art, though usually as bit-part players in classical allegory or bucolic landscape. But can we identify any London street trees?

Of course, until the 19th century urban scenes were rare, and, just as London took its concept of street-tree planting from other European cities – indeed, from artistic depictions of them – so it is to other nations' art we must look first.

The Dutch took to documenting their landscape, including towns and cities, earlier than others. Some incredible glimpses of street trees and arboricultural practices can be seen in the work of artists like Meindert Hobbema and Jan van der Heyden.

Many art students will have had the principles of perspective explained to them through Hobbema's 'The Avenue at Middelharnis' from 1689, which depicts a long, straight road lined with a regular, receding avenue of trees.

It's difficult to be certain of the species, but Poplar or Elm would be good candidates. They have been managed to attain height without being overburdened with foliage, perhaps to clearly demarcate the road and act as a landmark in the flat Dutch landscape.

'The Avenue at Middelharnis' can be seen in the National Gallery along with another unwitting masterpiece of Dutch arboreal painting from 1660, 'View of the Westerkerk, Amsterdam' by Jan van der Heyden,

Left: Hobbema's 'The Avenue at Middelharnis' depicts an early horticulturalist at work in a tree nursery on the right

Above: Van der Heyden's 'View of the Westerkerk, Amsterdam' – note the newly planted saplings in protective boxes complete with fly-posters

depicting street trees in paved areas along a canal. Not only does this painting capture a fascinating urban scene still recognisable to us; it also tantalisingly shows newly planted street trees!

Again, difficult to tell, but I'm fairly sure there are two distinct species, and at a guess I'd say they are mostly Elms. The newly planted trees, in the left foreground, are protected by wooden boxing, complete with fly-posters, around their young trunks.

Fast forward a couple of centuries to the Impress- ionists, and it was their depictions of mature Planes on late-19th-century tree-lined Parisian boulevards that so inspired London's first street-tree plantings. One of Camille Pissarro's series on Boulevard Montmartre, 'Boulevard Montmartre at Night' from 1897, is in the National Gallery. Lesser known but equally striking are Gustave Caillebotte's Parisian street scenes of the same period.

Pissarro spent two extended periods in London, painting the suburbs of Sydenham and Norwood in the 1870s, and returning in 1897 to produce 'Bath Road, Chiswick', complete with unidentifiable street tree saplings, now in Oxford's Ashmolean Museum.

That most famous Impressionist Claude Monet also spent time in London, capturing newly planted Plane trees in 'The Thames Below Westminster' of 1871 (see page 28).

The British artist John Atkinson Grimshaw, meanwhile, best known for his atmospheric night scenes, painted a remarkable view of Westminster in 1880 from a similar viewpoint to Monet's, nine years earlier. 'Reflections on the Thames', a very different piece, clearly shows a Plane protected by a wrought-iron tree guard.

In modern art, Keith Coventry, one of the YBAs (Young British Artists), known for his interest in social issues, has made numerous casts in bronze of vandalised urban trees, often street trees.

Who will be the first artist to depict one of London's Dawn Redwoods or Peanut Butter Trees?

Right: 'Drysdale Street, N1' by Keith Coventry, 2012

Far right: A detail of 'Reflections on the Thames' by John Atkinson Grimshaw, 1880

CAUCASIAN WINGNUT

Pterocarya fraxinifolia 🍁✩✩✩✩

The big wide tree with dangly bits, found in Bermondsey, Tufnell Park, Lisson Grove and at the Angel.

Islington is the best place for Wingnuts. It would seem a pioneering tree officer had a penchant for these trees and snuck them into many unlikely corners around the borough.

A tree that is wider than it is high, it needs enough room to truly show off – a rare luxury in London, and a potential drawback. Perhaps the best example of a Wingnut's grand potential can be seen in Tufnell Park, on the corner of St. George's Avenue and Carleton Road: a tree quite impossibly broad.

The Caucasian Wingnut is a native of a region around the Black Sea, where it apparently grows in mixed forest, something I find hard to comprehend, given its dense, spreading canopy, and habit of suckering profusely – evident with trees in London if left untended.

Wingnuts are named for their small nuts, surrounded by bracts, which hang in long conspicuous clusters up to 50 cm long. These distinctive fruits are also the best way to distinguish this species from the Tree of Heaven (see page 32), a species with very similar pinnate leaves (meaning, comprised of many leaflets).

Islington's trees are now mature, and many have been cut back severely in order to work in tight spots that with hindsight may not have been the best locations. A heavily pruned specimen at the Angel guards the entrance to Camden Passage.

Other boroughs are catching on, though. A stretch of Edgware Road around Lisson Grove in Westminster is lined with Wingnuts, and a street in Bermondsey, Wilson Grove is home to some big trees. These were planted in 1987 following the Great Storm that decimated trees across the city, including many on this street.

Wilson Grove represents Ada Salter's (see page 36) vision for model housing, and was formerly planted with Trees of Heaven. I wonder if the hasty planter of these post-storm trees mistook their large pinnate leaves for that species.

It's a street tree I hope we will see more of in the future, because the Caucasian Wingnut is a stunner.

Above: One of the Wilson Grove, Bermondsey trees, now so large it is blocking the pavement

Right: A splendid tree on the corner of Dalmeny Road and Carleton Road in Tufnell Park, surrounded by suckering shoots

THE ORNAMENTAL PEARS

Pyrus spp. 🍁🍁☆☆☆

Pears are present but infrequent street trees in London – apart from the Chanticleer, described on the next pages, that is – and perhaps deserve reappraisal. There are hundreds of varieties of orchard pears, beautiful large trees with stunning blossom and an autumn fruit bounty, but these are virtually never planted, because unloved fruits are just left to fall and rot. Understandably, local authorities are wary of planting trees that could cause slippery pavements, complaints from residents, legal bills or an increase in vermin.

Orchard pears are all cultivated varieties of *P. communis*. Could one develop an ornamental variety, producing glorious blossom and inconsequential fruits ideally suited for street planting?

The nearest the horticultural industry has come to this ideal pear is **Beech Hill** (*P. communis* '**Beech Hill**'), a cultivar of the dessert pear. It has lovely spring blossom leading to smallish, inedible fruits. These can be produced in such quantity that more than one tree on a street can cause pear-y mush in October, so it is now rare.

One or two other pears are present in even fewer numbers and might be regarded as also-rans. **Sand Pear** (*P. pyrifolia*) is an unusual, and somewhat controversial, Chinese species also known as the **Nashi Pear**, a crisp fruit that may be familiar to some. Good spring blossom leads to large apple-like fruits. One street planted with them, St John's Villas in Holloway, featured on the *Vanessa Feltz Show* after passions surrounding their car-bombing fruits ran so high. Now the council harvests the fruits each autumn, and residents use them for culinary purposes, including home-brewed perry.

The rather lovely **Weeping Pear** (*P. salicifolia* '**Pendula**'), usually restricted to old gardens, has made it onto the street in Kennington. It is a small cultivar of the Asian Willow-Leaved Pear with attractive silvery leaves and white spring blossom. It could be a useful street tree for a very narrow lane.

Finally, the handsome **Snow Pear** (*P. nivalis*) may be spotted in one or two corners. It is a characterful pear with attractive blossom and foliage, but again, problematic fruit.

Above: The large fruit of a Sand Pear on St John's Villas, Holloway

Right above: An example of '**Beech Hill**', Fann Street, in the City

Right below: Flowers and foliage of Snow Pear in Hackney

Far right: An apparently well-loved Weeping Pear on Claylands Road near the junction with Clapham Road in Vauxhall, its tree pit well cared for

CHANTICLEER PEAR

Pyrus calleryana 'Chanticleer' 🍁 🍁 🍁 🍁 🍁

A Marmite tree. Found all over town, from Brixton to Wembley.

This tree is loved and loathed in equal measure. In its favour, **'Chanticleer'**, like **'Bradford'**, another similar cultivar of the Asian Callery Pear, is virtually guaranteed to thrive and, at least when young, is a good low-maintenance choice. The other view is that these are uninteresting, overplanted trees which could be storing up problems for the future.

The non-cultivar Callery Pear is one of the most common street trees in New York – the 'Survivor Tree' from the 9/11 attacks on the World Trade Center is one. But a former NYC urban forester told me they are no longer planted there, as they've proved to be invasive, and older trees have a tendency to split.

London's trees tend to be young, so this latter problem has not yet surfaced; it could be due to colder American winters. As for their invasiveness, in our current climate self-seeding has not become a problem and, with just these cultivars present, fertile seed tends not to be produced. Mix them up with some non-cultivar Callery Pears and it could be a different story, though...

Chanticleers are renowned for their toughness and suitability for traffic-choked streets. They also retain a neat pyramidal shape, they don't get too large, and they keep their glossy leaves well into November when they can turn attractive shades of gold and orange. In fact, they are one of the last trees to turn, some still going strong well into December.

In more continental climates with warmer summers and cooler winters, Chanticleer Pears are renowned for their abundant and attractive spring blossom – which smells less attractive – followed by large amounts of inconspicuous brown berries rather than large, juicy pears.

In London some years, flowering is better than others, and in poor years fruits are few and far between, but a small rise in temperature could change that. So we could see consistently better blossom and more autumn colour in the future.

My own view is this is a dull tree. For consistent shape there are much better trees available: we could plant fastigiate Hornbeam, an avenue of which can be memorable. For spring flowers and autumn interest, cherries are peerless.

In the borough of Westminster, whole streets have been adorned with Chanticleer Pears, most notably Oxford Street. In comparison, Paris' main shopping street, Boulevard Haussman, is lined with splendid Plane trees, while Berlin's Unter den Linden is famed, and named for, its Limes.

Of all London's streets Oxford Street should surely have more ambitious planting.

Right: Looking east down Oxford Street on a March morning captures the Chanticleers at their very fleeting best: laden with blossom

ARRABELLA'S TREE

On Oxford Street in October 2016, a
small, golden-leaved tree appeared
outside Debenhams. In the note
attached, 7-year-old Arrabella
Cornelius announced that she had
bought this Field Maple with her
pocket money to fill the vacant tree
pit. (Here is her father bedding it in
under the cloak of darkness.)

Arrabella and her dad made
it onto breakfast TV, the Twitter-
sphere lauded 'a little individu-
alism in a somewhat Orwellian
world', but a month later her little
tree's glorious stand against the
Chanticleer Pear monoculture was
vanquished – uprooted, according
to the council, to a Marylebone
park.

THE OAKS

Quercus spp. ★★★☆☆

There are a large number of oak species, many with typical, easily identifiable lobed leaves. Others, though, are evergreen, and some confound easy identification – but all have acorns, although some years bring a bigger crop than others.

English Oak (*Quercus robur*) is the most frequent street oak, and along with its similar sibling, **Sessile Oak** (*Quercus petrea*) is described overleaf. Here, then, are some of the other, less frequent oaks that have made it streetside.

Several North American species are found, the most frequent being the handsome **Red Oak** (*Q. rubra*), a fairly common large species with big leaves, more angular than those of English Oak. In Red Oak's native lands, it will turn a magnificent scarlet in the autumn, as its name suggests, but our climate does not seem to inspire. While reds might be hinted at, in London it tends to head into the brown end of the spectrum.

Another North American with a promising name is **Scarlet Oak** (*Q. coccinea*) which does indeed turn scarlet in the autumn. It is quite unusual, though, and may be mistaken for the more frequent **Pin Oak** (*Q. palustris*). It has deeply incised leaves, each lobe of which ends in a distinct needle-like pin. This tree is reliably red in the autumn and can be quite dazzling, but it is a weaker, less handsome tree than the Red Oak, and does not yet appear to thrive in every London location.

The other Oaks you may encounter are Eurasian and more or less evergreen. Of these, **Holm Oak** (*Q. ilex*) is the most frequent, and the most familar. Mediterranean in origin, it thrives to such a degree that it commonly seeds itself in London, and these saplings can be mistaken for Holly, as the juvenile leaves are similarly spiky. A handsome tree that could be more widely planted, as Kingston town centre shows.

Turkey Oak (*Q. cerris*) is occasional. It is a huge, semi-evergreen tree, a good example of which can be seen on Lewisham High Street opposite the hospital.

The charming **Cork Oak** (*Q. suber*) is also present but very rare.

AN OAK FROM SW6?

Some oaks can interbreed, producing intersting hybrids. One of these is the **Fulham Oak** (*Q. x hispanica* **'Fulhamensis'**), a cross between Cork and Turkey Oaks. Called Fulham Oak by an 18th-century nursery based in SW6, it might make a good street tree. This acorn is on a young tree in the grounds of Fulham Palace.

Left above: Leaves of a Red Oak live up to the name at More London, Tooley Street

Left below: Pin Oak leaves on Oakhill Road in Hampstead

Far left: One of the Kingston town centre Holm Oaks on Clarence Street

ENGLISH OAK

Quercus robur   🍁 🍁 🍁 ☆ ☆

A mighty street tree of the future? Found in Forest Hill, Ilford, Pimlico and South Kensington.

English Oak is actually a relatively unusual street tree, a surprise considering the remarkable ancient specimens to be found across London from Richmond Park to Epping Forest. It should be more widely planted: not only is it a large native tree that plays host to an army of animals, birds and invertebrates; it is also a national icon that ought to be seen in the capital.

It seems appropriate to reintroduce oak trees to our streets wherever we can. They are beautiful, important trees much loved by many human and other city dwellers. Both our native oak trees are present in London: **Pedunculate**, or English, Oak (*Q. robur*), with stalkless leaves and stalked acorns, is the more common. The other species, **Sessile Oak** (*Q. petrea*), is very similar, but has leaves on stalks, while its acorns are stalkless.

Oaks can live for hundreds of years, longer than much of London's built environment, so in a few places street trees can be found that pre-date the city's Victorian expansion. These old sentinels probably started life in a field, estate, garden, or even a wood now long gone, and can be seen particularly in London's outer boroughs.

Excellent examples of remnant oaks can be seen right across town. The Little Gaynes Lane Oak in Upminster is thought to be 330 years old and could be the oldest street tree in London. An old tree on Oakhill Road in Hampstead pre-dates the Edwardian houses, and in Ealing the Carlton Road tree sits right in the middle of the road.

At one time Oaks were extremely common in London and the dominant woodland tree but, much prized for timber and with a low tolerance of industrial pollution, most had disappeared by the end of the 19th century.

More recent examples of planned street planting are starting to appear. On the Strand outside Charing Cross Station an oak appears to be surviving despite being next to a busy road and surrounded by paved surfaces. Others can be seen outside Pimlico Station, again thriving, and in the City on Fenchurch Street.

A SURPRISING OAK

A newly popular cultivar beginning to be planted frequently is the uniformly upright **'Koster'** clone, also known as the **Cypress Oak**. This is an ideal oak for a tight spot or, for that matter, an elegant avenue or an architectural planting scheme. They are starting to appear in locations across town, I bumped into this parade of trees outside South Kensington Station.

Above: A fabulous old Pedunculate Oak tree sits in the middle of a roundabout on Lawrie Park Avenue in Sydenham, once no doubt a constituent of the Great North Wood

Right: A young Pedunculate Oak street tree example on Fenchurch Street in the City of London

FALSE ACACIA OR BLACK LOCUST

Robinia pseudoacacia 🍁🍁🍁🍁

The tree that gave its name to that suburban stereotype, Acacia Avenue. Found all over from Dollis Hill to Streatham, and Bexley to Southall.

An attractive, much-planted North American tree, False Acacia has been here long enough to fit in well into our urban landscape, having been introduced back in 1636. John Evelyn wrote that it 'deserves a place among our avenue trees, adorning our walks with their exotic leaf and sweet flowers'.

Like a true acacia, False Acacia, or Black Locust as this tree is known in its native USA, has attractive compound or pinnate leaves, in this case comprised of 9-19 loosely oval leaflets. A true acacia, on the other hand, such as Mimosa (see page 14), would have many more, much smaller feathery leaves.

False Acacias flower briefly, sometimes copiously, in late May to early June, and have hanging clusters, or racemes, of fragrant, creamy-white, pea-like flowers. Bees love them and, in some countries, they are the source of acacia honey. The flowers are followed by leguminous seed pods that can stay on the tree through the winter.

Perhaps the most distinctive feature of this medium-to-large tree is its gaunt, somewhat twisted silhouette, giving it an aged and char-acterful appearance. It reminds me of trees depicted in 17th-century landscape painting.

An unfortunate characteristic is its brittleness, leading to a habit of dropping branches. I've witnessed a branch fall from an old tree on a still, mild day without any obvious external pressure. As a result, False Acacias are less favoured these days, but similar trees, like Honey Locust (see page 98), are increasingly planted, sometimes in close proximity to False Acacia.

Several cultivars might be encountered, including the very occasional, and fastigiate, **'Pyramidalis'**; the mop-topped **'Umbrac-ulifera'** and the less-leafy **'Unifoliola'** may be seen. A newly planted tree is likely to be the **'Bessoniana'** cultivar, with a more rounded habit and bright green foliage.

GOLDEN FALSE ACACIA

The most frequent False Acacia cul-tivar must be **'Frisia'**, and with good reason. It has striking golden yellow foliage that persists throughout the seasons (many golden-leaved cultivars tend to revert to green as the summer progresses). This fine example can be seen on Danby Road, Peckham.

Above: Flowers and leaves in Blythe Road, Shepherd's Bush

Right: A tree with unusually abundant flowers in May, Elgar Close, Deptford

GIANT REDWOOD

Sequoiadendron giganteum 🍁 ☆☆☆☆

Big Daddy. Found in Edgware and Kilburn.

Yes, there are Giant Redwoods on London's streets!

This is one of the world's largest trees, reaching a height of 94.8 metres (311 feet), and a diameter of 8.2 metres (27 feet). It can live for 3,500 years.

The Victorians and Edwardians were fascinated by them – understandably – and set about planting avenues and groves of them on country estates that are now magnificent sights. One such Edwardian avenue, in Edgware, lined the approach to a large house. The house is now the North London Collegiate School: the driveway became a suburban avenue, Canons Drive, and, rather wonderfully, the Redwoods were kept.

A trip to Canons Drive is well worth it, to see not only the amazing trees but also an aspiring early-20th-century garden suburb. This is, make no mistake, a much-sought-after place to live.

The trees were planted in 1910, and in just over a century have already attained magnificent proportions. The avenue is dominated by Giant Redwoods, but at least one Coast Redwood and several **Deodar Cedars** (*Cedrus deodara*) are present.

Another grove of younger trees can be found on the corner of Fernhead Road and Kilburn Lane. These are planted directly into the pavement, unlike on Canons Drive, where the trees are part of a broad verge. Despite this difficult situation, the Kilburn trees appear to be doing just fine, suggesting Giant Redwoods could be considered for more frontline positions.

Like Dawn Redwoods (see page 128), Giant Redwoods are rare, and restricted to a small native territory, in this case the Sierra Nevada mountains of central California.

AN EVEN TALLER TREE

Another giant tree from California, the **Coast Redwood** (*Sequoia sempervirens*) is the world's tallest tree, with one individual reaching an almost unimaginable 115.5 metres (379 feet).

Similar to the Giant Redwood in many ways, it can be told apart by its leaves. Giant Redwoods have green shoots clothed in scale-like leaves; Coast Redwoods have more variable leaves, ranging from scales to needle-like growths. Besides at least one on Canons Drive, there is an example, not looking terribly well, on Sedding Street in Chelsea, leading up to the Cadogan Hall north of Sloane Square.

Above: A newly planted **'Pygmaeum'** cultivar (a slow-growing dwarf form) on Worship Street in Shoreditch marks the border between Hackney and the City of London

Right: The awe-inspiring avenue of Giant Redwoods on Canons Drive in Edgware

WHAT STREET TREES DOESN'T LONDON HAVE... YET?

'Lemons.' That's what one urban forester told me he'd like to see planted on London's streets. It's surprising, he went on, what would grow in a sunny, south-west-facing spot. *Citrus x limon*, he thought, would thrive.

After all, in the future London is only going to get warmer and drier, and the urban heat island effect means the city centre can often be more than 10^0 warmer than the surrounding countryside, particularly at night. Urban foresters are already selecting species which might once have seemed exotic, in order to build in resilience to the effect of climate change. Street trees like Crêpe Myrtle (see page 101), Olive (page 132) or Hibiscus (page 100) would have been

unheard-of in London even a few decades ago. Less glamorous trees like Nettle Trees (page 66) and Willow-leaved Sandthorns (page 104) are all about coping with hot and dry conditions too.

It has been suggested that the climate of parts of the Balkan peninsula, such as the southern Carpathian mountains in Romania, and the Balkan and Rhodope ranges in Bulgaria, more accurately mimics the conditions found on London's streets that that of the surrounding countryside.

Nurseries and urban foresters are already looking here to build up the gene pool of familiar trees and to add new species to the palette, so don't be surprised if you notice more oaks, including **Hungarian Oak** (*Quercus frainetto*), and some unusual conifers such as **Macedonian Fir** (*Abies x borisii-regis*), appearing in the coming years.

As well as the Balkans, London, with its world city status, should look to other international cities with similar, or slightly warmer, climates: San Francisco, Seattle and Portland in the Western USA, for example; Melbourne, Wellington and Christchurch in the southern hemisphere.

On the evidence of these cities' planting, exciting tree choices we could look forward to might include some of the following.

Norfolk Island Pine (*Araucaria heterophylla*), may be familiar as a very regular houseplant, but it will actually become a large tree. It's already much used on city streets in warmer places including Nice and Auckland. Tantalisingly, a large tree can be found thriving on an estate near the Elephant and Castle.

Another contender is **Peruvian Pepper Tree** (*Schinus molle*), the source of 'pink peppercorns', much planted as a street tree in parts of California, including San Francisco. A single specimen is already doing fine on the street in Kennington (page 109).

Tree aficionados may be surprised to discover

that we don't yet have **True Service Trees** (*Sorbus domestica*) lining any London streets. A species that has recently been confirmed as a native, it's more usually seen in southern Europe. Like a giant Rowan (page 188), it's far longer-lived and produces larger fruits.

Also known as the New Zealand Christmas Tree, **Pohutukawas** (*Metrosideros excelsa*) are native to parts of the warmer North Island, growing into venerable trees that blaze with abundant bright red flowers in high summer (Christmastime down under).

Brisbane Box (*Lophostemon confertus*) is an Australian evergreen tree highly tolerant of the rigours of urban life. It is one of the most popular street trees in California and temperate parts of Australia.

Far left: A suburban street in the town of Iznagar in Cordoba province, Spain, lined with Lemon trees

Left: A Norfolk Island Pine in south London

Above: A Pohutukawa in Auckland, New Zealand

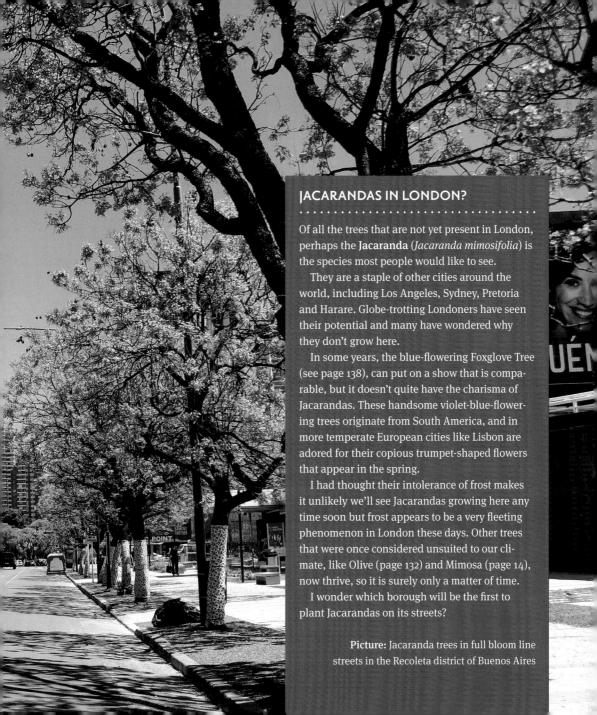

JACARANDAS IN LONDON?

Of all the trees that are not yet present in London, perhaps the **Jacaranda** (*Jacaranda mimosifolia*) is the species most people would like to see.

They are a staple of other cities around the world, including Los Angeles, Sydney, Pretoria and Harare. Globe-trotting Londoners have seen their potential and many have wondered why they don't grow here.

In some years, the blue-flowering Foxglove Tree (see page 138), can put on a show that is comparable, but it doesn't quite have the charisma of Jacarandas. These handsome violet-blue-flowering trees originate from South America, and in more temperate European cities like Lisbon are adored for their copious trumpet-shaped flowers that appear in the spring.

I had thought their intolerance of frost makes it unlikely we'll see Jacarandas growing here any time soon but frost appears to be a very fleeting phenomenon in London these days. Other trees that were once considered unsuited to our climate, like Olive (page 132) and Mimosa (page 14), now thrive, so it is surely only a matter of time.

I wonder which borough will be the first to plant Jacarandas on its streets?

Picture: Jacaranda trees in full bloom line streets in the Recoleta district of Buenos Aires

THE WILLOWS

Salix spp. 🍁☆☆☆☆

Serene water-loving trees found in Southwark.

Think of willows, and billowing waterside trees probably spring to mind. So it may not be surprising that willows are very rarely planted on our streets. As well as their thirst, willows are renowned for their fragility – indeed, one species, **Crack Willow,** recalls this feature in its Latin name, *Salix fragilis.* But this hasn't stopped Southwark tree planters: Crack Willows can be seen at Canada Water, where heavily pollarded examples line Maritime Street.

Not far away, on South Sea Street next to the huge expanse of Greenland Water, **Weeping Willows** (*S. x sepulcralis* '**Chrysocoma**') can be seen. Perhaps the loveliest and most easily recognised willow, they are far more often seen in parks and gardens than on the side of the road. But here they are in all their swishing loveliness. Certainly an interesting choice, and something that could be rather lovely where space allows, although you never know what may go on under that pavement-brushing canopy.

Weeping Willows are less prone to the snapping branches of other large willows, but they do require a lot of space to be fully appreciated. They could make an interesting roundabout feature or a fine avenue on a particularly broad street with a grass verge – a rare street tree environment in London.

The only other willow that has occasionally been planted is the distinctive **Corkscrew Willow** (*S. matsudana* '**Tortuosa**'). As one urban forester told me, this tree looks as if it has been electrocuted. Crazy, tortured twigs curl like a bad perm and sprout similarly twisted leaves. This is a fast-growing, short-lived tree, so probably not an ideal street tree. Willows are, it seems, destined to be forever rare.

Above: A Corkscrew Willow on Gambia Street near Tate Modern

Right: One of the Greenland Water trees on South Sea Street, Rotherhithe

THE ROWANS & WHITEBEAMS

Sorbus spp. 🍁🍁🍁🍁☆

All the species in the *Sorbus* genus are small trees with white flower cluster and berries, some more prominent than others. The leaf shapes are what set each species apart. Besides the three outlined over the next pages, there are others, less conspicuous but nevertheless noteworthy.

The bluntly named **Bastard Service Tree** (*S. x thuringiaca*) is a tree once much planted, but now apparently out of fashion. It is a hybrid of Rowan and Whitebeam, and has leaves shaped midway between the two. A large oval leaflet is followed by usually two pairs of smaller rowan-type leaflets. It has small bunches of orange-red berries and, most examples being the '**Fastigiata**' cultivar, with a tight, ascending crown, making for a fine winter silhouette.

Swedish Whitebeam (*S. x intermedia*) appears closest to regular Whitebeam, a variable species in its own right – there are several distinct and rare Whitebeams endemic to specific parts of the UK, from south Devon cliffs to Scottish islands. These are yet to make themselves known in London.

Swedish Whitebeam is a naturally occurring hybrid, with Rowan, Whitebeam and Wild Service heritage: its leaves are oval and deeply cut, it has smooth grey bark and orange-red berries. Popular as a street tree in the past – some old specimens may be seen – but it appears to be another tree out of fashion now.

Several other Sorbus species might be seen including the **Service Tree of Fontainebleau** (*S. latifolia*), another tree with a great name. Similar to Swedish Whitebeam, its leaves are slightly broader.

Look out for the neat **Chinese Scarlet Rowan** (*S. commixta*), with leaves turning a striking crimson in the autumn.

Above: Chinese Scarlet Rowan, Corbyn Street, Stroud Green

Right above: White berries of a **Kasmiri Rowan** (*S. cashmiriana*), Zoffany Street, Archway

Right below: Bastard Service Tree leaves showing separate leaflets, Danby Street, Peckham

Far right: A magnificent fastigiate Bastard Service Tree, Harrowby Street, Marylebone

WHITEBEAM

Sorbus aria 🍁🍁🍁☆☆

The subtle tree with white leaves found all over from Croydon to Hammersmith.

The lovely Whitebeam is a common smaller street tree, although it appears to be less planted now than in previous years. Whitebeams are right at home on chalk, and native trees might therefore still be found wild in parts of Croydon and Bromley. As with many *Sorbus* species, they don't appear to be in vogue right now.

As a native, and especially a London native, it is to be particularly encouraged, not least because of its importance for biodiversity – the number of insect and birds that make use of its leaves, flowers and berries.

The defining feature of this tree is the white undersides of its leaves, from which it gets its name (the 'beam' part is an old English word for tree). These downy white leaves, oval-shaped and finely serrated, become particularly apparent in the spring as the milky buds burst open. While they are not as showy as some trees' blossom, the Whitebeam's fresh, creamy leaves are still quite special.

In April bunches of creamy flowers arrive; visually they merge into the tree. From October red berries appear, popular with birds; by early December trees have usually been stripped bare. Whitebeams maintain a broad, rounded shape, and develop stout, smooth, grey-barked trunks that often show a distinct spiral twist and with a bit of imagination remind me of a Baobab tree.

There are several cultivars around: the most frequent, **'Lutescens'**, has the whitest new leaves; others include **'Magnifica'**, a more upright tree, and **'Majestica'**, with larger leaves, a good avenue of which can be seen lining Bedford Way, north of Russell Square in Bloomsbury.

Above: A mature tree with ripe berries and a twisted trunk on Tregaron Avenue, Crouch End

Right above: Emerging leaves, Arngask Street, Hither Green

Right middle: Fluffy flowers merge into the leaves of a tree on Bedford Way in Bloomsbury

Right below: Ripe red berries, Nichols Green, Ealing

Far right: A young tree coming into leaf, Giffin Street, Deptford

ROWAN OR MOUNTAIN ASH

Sorbus aucuparia 🍁🍁🍁🍁🍁

The red berry tree, common across the capital, from Tooting to Tottenham.

At the time of writing, Rowans are probably the most frequently newly planted street trees in London, bucking the trend set by many other *Sorbus* species. As one urban forester told me, if you plant a Rowan, chances are you will outlive it.

Rather like the old adage about no-one ever getting fired for buying IBM, Rowan is seen as a risk-free choice for virtually every situation. It's a tree that does not get too large, and, if it needs replacing, it won't take too long for the next tree to reach maturity. Oh, and it seems to manage with London street life. That said, Rowans are perhaps more suited to a slightly damper and cooler climate, which may account for their rather short life expectancy on our streets.

Rowans, or Mountain Ash, so named for the pinnately-compound leaves resembling those of Ash (see page 92), have a lot to recommend them. They are native, so good for biodiversity, as the insects seen around the flowers and birds around the berries will attest. The flowers are pleasant, if not in the same league as cherry, and the foliage can take on excellent autumn crimson and gold.

But the berries are the speciality. Produced in great abundance and ripening from late August, they can feed an army of blackbirds, goldfinches and, occasionally, waxwings well into January. Branches can be literally weighed down by them.

Over the years more and more cultivars have been introduced, most visibly with differing berry colours. The species is naturally blessed with a deep orange-red crop, but now yellow (**'Sunshine'** and **'Streetwise'**), orange (**'Golden Wonder'**), pinkish-white (**'Glowing Pink'**) and deep vermillion may be seen. **'Asplenifolia'**, meanwhile, has deeply serrated leaves and is very infrequent.

Undeniably, Rowan is a reliable tree for frontline service but, while it is loved by tree managers and the public alike, there are some less desirable things to consider. I mentioned that it is short-lived – 25 years would appear to be a good innings – and so, in my opinion, Rowans should not be planted if something larger or more long-lived could fill its tree-pit.

Like the overplanted Chanticleer Pear (page 168), Rowan could be considered overplanted. They are rather boring and their berries have an odd plasticky appearance, compounded by the synthetic colours of some cultivars.

I have seen a gap in an avenue of Planes filled by a hopeful Rowan sapling, which seems inappropriate to say the least; in just a few decades the Rowan is likely to have succumbed, while the large Planes surrounding it will have another 200 years left in them, and any new Plane will, unnecessarily, be 25 years behind its companions.

Right above: Newly planted Rowans in Ponders End

Right below: Ripe berries on a Japan Crescent, Crouch Hill tree

Far right: Rowan flowers on Morval Road, Brixton

WILD SERVICE TREE

Sorbus torminalis 🍁☆☆☆☆

The 'Chequers' tree. Found in Acton, Islington, Bloomsbury and Hackney.

A rare native of ancient woodlands, which can be found growing naturally in Highgate, Queens and Oxleas Woods, this is one of my very favourite trees. It was the species I, a singular, tree-obsessed child, most wanted to find: a flowering tree with distinctive leaves, and brown berries that are allegedly edible after being bletted – the term for the process of rotting through freezing and unfreezing.

I grew up in Kent, where I learned the local name for the fruit of Wild Service Trees was 'Chequers' and that, tantalisingly, pubs with this name were likely to be named after the fruit or the trees. Despite searching in the vicinity of several country inns, though, I never found any Wild Service Trees. So it was with considerable surprise that I bumped into a street tree outside a pub in north London, the mistakenly named Clarence Tavern in Stoke Newington. I've since found several more newly planted trees in Acton, Islington and Bloomsbury as well as others in Hackney.

Despite a natural penchant for shady woods it appears to be doing well on the street, and there one is able to examine it more closely. At the moment the trees are small, and I'm unsure how large they might become. I hope they'll be closer to the related Whitebeam than their other cousin, the Rowan.

The easiest way to recognise Wild Service Trees is by the distinctive leaves: spiky and palmate, somewhere between a Hawthorn and a maple, they turn golden orange through to scarlet in the autumn. In May, the blossom opens in clusters, and is similar to other related *Sorbus* species, but perhaps slightly whiter and more distinct than Whitebeam. Fat brown berries – the chequers – develop and can stay on the tree until the following spring after the leaves have disappeared.

I am hopeful it is a tree we might see in more boroughs in the future. It is native to the UK, and London is specifically within its natural distribution range, where it particularly seems to thrive on our clay soils. Wild Service Trees are interesting, attractive and unusual. They are part of this city's natural heritage, too, so more, please!

ROWAN, WHITEBEAMS AND SERVICE TREES OFFER LIQUID SUSTENANCE

There is a much-repeated myth that the Wild Service Tree's name is a corruption of *cerevisia*, the Latin word for beer, and that service berries were often used for this purpose. One ecologist, Patrick Roper, has made a study of this claim (which he says doesn't hold water), but he has discovered dozens of other Bacchanalian uses for *Sorbus* berries recorded down the centuries. Tantalising tipples include:

Aliziergeist – an *eau-de-vie* distilled from Wild Service berries in Germany and Austria

Cormé – a fermented wine-type beverage made with the berries of true Service in France

Diod griafol – a distillation of rowan berries from north Wales, said by John Evelyn to be 'incomparable'

Ryabina na konyake – a fortified drink from Belarus made with Rowan berries and brandy.

Many more are listed at:
rowanswhitebeamsandservicetrees.blogspot.com

Above top: Ripe chequers on the Stoke Newington tree outside the Clarence Tavern, Bouverie Road

Above: Distinctive leaves and blossom detail from a tree on St Peter's Way, off the Kingsland Road in Dalston

Right: Attractive autumn colouring on a Wilberforce Road, Finsbury Park tree

WHERE ARE THE GREAT STREET TREES OF LONDON?

For readers in a hurry, here's a round-up of some of the most remarkable street trees in this most remarkable of cities.

The Wembley Elm. A rare European White Elm on the corner of Harrow Road and Oakington Manor Drive. Wembley Central Tube station.

The Dulwich Caucasian Zelkova. At the corner of College Road and the South Circular. Nearest station, West Dulwich.

The Hampstead Plane. Perhaps the largest street tree in London. Christchurch Hill near the corner with Well Walk. Hampstead Tube station.

The Edgware Giant Redwoods. Canons Drive, midway between Edgware and Canons Park Tube stations.

The Lewisham Black Mulberry. One of London's very infrequent Mulberry street trees. Pine Tree Way (inexplicably), a short walk from Lewisham Station.

The High Court Dawn Redwoods. Carey Street, to the rear of the Royal Courts of Justice on the Strand. Holborn, Chancery Lane or Temple Tube stations.

The Archway Chinese or Lacebark Elms. Including the largest example in the UK of this rare species. Magdala Avenue, opposite the entrance to the Whittington Hospital. Archway Tube station.

The Herne Hill Yoshino Cherries. Several streets just a short walk from Herne Hill Station: Stradella Road is good, but Winterbrook Road is best.

The Embankment Planes. The first street trees to be systematically planted. Embankment Tube station.

The Finsbury Park Almond. A pink-flowering Almond with a corkscrew trunk on the corner of Stroud Green Road and Tollington Park. Finsbury Park Tube station.

The Ealing 'Elephant' Oak. Legend has it that the old oak tree in the middle of Carlton Road marks the grave of an elephant. Ealing Broadway Tube station.

The Kensington Postbox Plane. An Edwardian post-box is gradually being consumed on the corner of Drayton Gardens and Priory Walk. Nearest Tube, South Kensington.

The Putney Sweet Chestnut. A very old and stout tree using the full width of the pavement on Heathview Gardens. East Putney Tube station is 20 minutes away.

The Upminster Oak. A contender for London's oldest street tree, the 350-year-old oak is on Little Gaynes Lane. A short hike from Upminster Tube station.

The Pimlico Mimosa. Visit Lupus Street in February for fabuous blossom with a gorgeous scent. Nearest Tube: Pimlico.

The Marylebone Elm. A surviving Huntingdon Elm on Marylebone High Street. Baker Street Tube station.

The Chiswick 'Baobab' Plane. A rare and distinctive London Plane cultivar. Short and very fat, it can be seen on Coniston Close. Chiswick Station.

The Croydon Oak pollards. A fine row of remnant oak trees line Oaks Road. Coombe Lane tram stop.

The Brixton Plane. Brixton's landmark tree shades Windrush Square. Brixton Tube station.

Left: The Finsbury Park Almond
Above: The Kensington Postbox Plane

JAPANESE PAGODA TREE

Styphnolobium japonicum, formerly *Sophora japonica* 🍁🍁

A shy tree. Seen in Archway, the City and Homerton.

Despite its name, Japanese Pagoda Trees actually originate from China and Korea, but have long been associated with Japan where they are known as Scholar's Tree.

It is a popular street tree in Paris and New York, and is now being planted more frequently in London. It has similar pinnate leaves to a False Acacia (see page 174) or a Honey Locust (see page 98), for which it could be easily mistaken.

The simplest way to positively identify this tree is to look at the young branches, which retain smooth dark green bark for several years before becoming rougher and light brown with age.

There are remarkably few mature trees in London, despite it being introduced as early as 1753. Indeed, that original tree can still be seen at Kew, where it has become completely recumbent.

Pagoda Trees will produce bunches, or racemes, of aromatic white flowers in late August and September. These are pea-like (or leguminous) and similar to those of False Acacia, but the racemes are erect rather than drooping. Perhaps a reason for its relative rarity here is that the flowers are not produced as easily as they are on trees in Paris, for instance.

This has not deterred a recent flush of planting in several parts of town, suggesting urban foresters are hopeful Japanese Pagoda Trees will be freer with their blossom as the climate warms. When they do flower, they can be spectacular but, as well as being a shy bloomer, the species is also known for waiting at least 30 years before even a single flower is produced.

This is a future-proof tree, planted for the long-term, and one to look forward to in a decade or two.

Above: A newly planted tree outside Archway Tube station

Right above: A tree outside Homerton Overground station in perhaps its first blossom season

Right below: Even rarer than flowers are the ripening seed pods. Seen here on a Byng Place, Bloomsbury tree

Far right: Pretty white flowers produced in branched racemes on a tree on Gresham Street in the City

THE LIMES

Tilia spp. ✤✤✤✤✤

Although we call them Limes, this is a peculiarly British name for a group of trees known to the rest of the world as Lindens, a group that has nothing whatsoever to do with citrus fruit. Several Lime species can be seen on London's streets, many of which are now actively planted.

The most familar tree must be the **Common Lime** of suburban avenues, which is decribed overleaf. Here, though, are some of the other Limes encountered around town.

We have two native Limes, both present: the **Large-leaved** (*T. platyphyllos*) and the **Small-leaved Lime** (*T. cordata*). The Small-leaved species makes an attractive medium-sized tree with a regular, high-domed crown similar to Common Lime, but more restrained. It suffers less from aphid infestation and does not sucker. This is the source of lime wood, the most sought-after material for decorative carving, and the wood used by Grinling Gibbons, that great 17th-century sculptor whose carved lime work can be seen in St Paul's Cathedral. Most London trees are the **'Greenspire'** cultivar. You may also see **'Rancho'**, a smaller tree in every respect, and **'Winter Orange'**, with bright orange twigs for winter interest.

There are several intriguing species with less-rounded leaves which can be confusing too. Of these, **Mongolian Lime** (*T. mongolica*) is most frequent. It has distinctive serrated leaf edges and promises to make an attractive street tree with a dense, somewhat unkempt crown. A few trees have been planted on the appropriately named Linden Grove on the north-west side of Nunhead Cemetery. Rare, but similar is **Henry's Lime** (*T. henryana*), examples of which can be seen in Hackney and Kentish Town.

Another attractive medium-to-large lime with a rounded crown is **Silver Lime** (*T. tomentosa*). On a hot, 30°-plus day, this tree will twist its leaves to direct the white – or silver – undersides at the sun in order to shield itself from the scorching effects. Not good for bees, though, for whom the flowers are so attractive they can cause addicted insects to keep returning to the same tree even after the flowers have finished, ultimately leading to bees dying of exhaustion.

Above: A young Silver Lime laden with flowers on Mayford Road, Balham

Right above: Leaves and flowers of a Mongolian Lime on Linden Grove, Nunhead

Right below: Attractive fringed foliage of Henry's Lime, Kentish Town

Far right: A Small-leaved Lime on Lupus Street, outside the Pimlico Academy

COMMON LIME

Tilia x europaea 🌳🌳🌳🌳🌳

The original avenue tree. Frequenting upmarket postcodes from Dulwich, Richmond and Balham to Ruislip, Finchley and Chingford.

Before Planes became synonymous with London in the late 19th century, Limes were the urban tree of choice, and not just in Britain: since the 17th century one of Berlin's most celebrated landmarks is its wide central boulevard Unter den Linden – lined with Lime trees to this day.

Limes were much favoured for their ability to be cut back hard year after year, and for pleaching, the practice of training trees to form avenues, screens or tunnels. Pleached Limes are still seen in the grounds of stately homes and private gardens, and very occasionally in the city too. Head to Canada Square at Canary Wharf, or Courtenay Square in Kennington to see unusual urban examples of pleached Limes.

The common Lime is a hybrid of two increasingly rare-in-the-wild native species, the **Small-leaved Lime** (*T. cordata*), and the **Large-leaved** (*T. platyphyllos*). In size its fresh, mid-green, heart-shaped leaves are midway between the two. Left to its own devices, this tree can become larger than either parent – up to 50 metres – and live for at least 300 years.

Limes are also easy to propagate from cuttings or suckers thrown out around the base – a gift for Victorian and Edwardian nurserymen, who could rapidly provide vigorous, uniform trees for whole new districts springing up around London.

As London became larger, busier and dirtier, neat walks framed by manicured Limes gave way to busy, clogged, macadamed roads, and later in the 19th century the first systematic planting of street trees in central London was almost entirely of pollution-toler-

ant Plane trees. Limes remained popular in the quieter, more affluent parts of town, and it is in these leafier outer boroughs where avenues of well-groomed trees laid out over a hundred years ago can still be found.

An avenue of Limes like that opposite is a wonderful, quintessentially English sight. I feel we should protect these examples of past urban planning and I would even suggest we plant more of them. In the future, we may well have reduced our dependency on privately-owned, infrequently-used cars cluttering streets, and handsome Lime-tree-lined avenues could once more come into their own.

Nowadays, though, Lime is very infrequently planted. It is no longer fashionable nor cost-effective to keep trees quite as immaculately pruned as our forebears did. Without this, the tree's fast growth means greater leaf area, and more honeydew.

By way of compensation, the abundant flowers of common Lime open in mid-June and are wonderfully fragrant. For some, though, this heralds an annual ordeal: Lime flower pollen produces allergic reactions for many hay fever sufferers and, along with Plane and Birch, it is one of the worst offenders.

Above right: Crouch Hall Road in Crouch End is a typical well-manicured Lime avenue

Below right: Fresh green, heart-shaped leaves on Langham Road, Teddington

HONEYDEW, THE BANE OF MOTORISTS

That sticky secretion that blackens cars and pavements is known as honeydew. But this miasma is not in fact produced by the tree, but rather dumped on bonnets, windscreens and pavements by the rich aphid life it supports. So technically, it's aphid poo.

THE ELMS

Ulmus spp. 🍁🍁☆☆☆

Rare survivors. Found in Archway, Wembley, Marylebone and Nine Elms, of course.

Elm street trees have never been common in London, but before the Dutch Elm Disease epidemic of the 1970s they were surely more frequent than now, perhaps more so in parks rather than on our streets. These days there are a few notable mature street trees, and some newly planted disease-resistant varieties.

Dutch Elm Disease was an arboreal disaster, wiping out 20 million trees in the UK in only a few years – but also a cautionary tale. As pest and diseases are lining up to have a go at our Ash, Plane and Oak trees, to name just three, there is every possibility that another species could succumb to a similar fate.

The surviving elms should be cherished, then, not only for their links to our urban landscape of the past, but also as a possible source of resistant genes for future generations. Two old elm street trees have 'Great Tree of London' status: membership of a select group of 61 trees deemed to be extra-special. The first 41 trees on this list were voted for by the public following the Great Storm of 1987, and the rest were added in 2008.

First on the list is the magnificent Marylebone Elm, a huge example of a **Huntingdon Elm** (*U. x hollandica* **'Vegeta'**), once a common species throughout the east of England. The other is the Wembley Elm, a rare example of a **European White Elm** (*U. laevis*), another old tree and a local landmark, to be found outside The Arch bar on the corner of Oakington Manor Drive and the Harrow Road, in the shadow of Wembley Stadium.

Elms all have asymmetric, pointed-oval leaves, with one side more lobed than the other at the stalk. They also have distinctive flat, round, winged seeds or samara. Beyond that, there is a lot of variation between species, causing elms to be notoriously difficult to positively identify. Some have small leaves, others large and more serrated; others' leaves are smooth, while there are also variants with downy undersides.

Disease-resistant varieties include **New Horizon** (*U.* **'New Horizon'**), a cultivar raised in the US, and now the most frequently planted. A fine row can be seen on Queen Victoria Street in the City outside the Salvation Army Headquarters. **Princeton Elm** (*U. americana* **'Princeton'***)* can be found among the Planes and Limes of Camberwell Grove, and the **Golden Elm** (*U. x hollandica* **'Dampieri Aurea'**) is dotted around town. Down at Nine Elms, the original nine trees have been restored, the last pair of *U.* **'Lutece'** being planted in 2019. See them on Nine Elms Lane opposite the new US embassy.

Archway is an unlikely elm hotspot, with some splendid large trees, mostly rare **Chinese Lacebark Elms** (*U. parvifolia*): Magdala Avenue opposite the Whittington Hospital is lined with them, and others can be seen on Archway and Bredgar Roads.

Right: An upright Golden Elm, looking less golden in late summer, on Portobello Road, Notting Hill

Far right: The Marylebone Elm, Marylebone High Street

WANT TO SEE ELMS? HEAD TO THE COAST

To see Elms in all their glory and variation requires a day trip to Brighton. Because of its location between the South Downs and the sea, Brighton has been protected from the ravages of Dutch Elm Disease, a fungus passed from tree to tree by a beetle that has yet to make it over the hills or cross the English Channel. Brighton is home to 17,000 Elms and the National Elm Collection.

See *brightonelmtrees.com* for more details.

JAPANESE ZELKOVA OR KEYAKI

Zelkova serrata 🍁☆☆☆☆

A surprisingly rare Japanese tree found in Camden Town, Pimlico, Chiswick and Croydon.

No self-respecting guidebook could be complete without at least one 'Z', and in a tree book that means Zelkova. There are two species in this wonderfully named genus to be found in London, one from the Caucasus, the other from Japan.

 Caucasian Zelkova (*Z. carpinifolia*) is a large, spreading tree with a mass of upward-sweeping branches, virtually unheard-of as a street tree. A single, old specimen can be found in Dulwich on the corner of College Road and the South Circular, but it has been very brutally hacked about.

 The **Japanese Zelkova**, known as **Keyaki** in Japan, is by contrast the species more likely to be en- countered, but even this smaller and very elegant tree is remarkably unusual.

 It may be that it gets confused with other species. Young trees might be mistaken for cherries: they have similar but smaller and more deeply serrated leaves. This appears to be what has happened in Binns Road, Chiswick, where a lonely Keyaki punctuates a row of Winter-Flowering Cherries. They might also be confused with fastigiate Hornbeams or Elms, to which Zelkovas are closely related.

 When you have positively identified a couple, these trees become unmistakeable, and indeed sought-after. Keyaki wood is a deep chestnut brown and prized for traditional furniture in Japan, while bonsai enthusiasts rate Keyaki as an excellent subject for that ancient art of tree-torturing.

 As well as the fine examples pictured here, a pair of Keyaki trees can be seen tucked away in Pimlico on Causton Street.

Above: An autumnal tree outside the Koko nightclub across the road from Mornington Crescent Tube station in Camden Town

Right: This being, alphabetically, the last tree in the book, it is appropriate to include an example from one of London's furthest reaches. This example graces New Addington's Central Parade in Croydon

This book is an introduction to the trees on London's streets, there are over 350 species and cultivars present, so there are many I have not been able to include. The list of trees on our streets is only set to increase, but four notable species that are of particular interest, and likely to be more visible in the future, are described here.

Species become popular street trees for all sorts of reasons. Some are developed and introduced by the horticultural industry, such as the ornamental cherries (see page 154) and apples (page 122). Others are selected from wild populations found in Asia or North America, like the Persian Silk Tree (page 38) or the Honey Locust (page 98). Yet more are great rarities that may need protection in the wild; a strategy to save these species, like the Dawn Redwood (page 128), is to introduce them into the horticultural industry.

These four very different species come from each of these categories.

A tree developed for horticulture is the peculiar *x Chitalpa tashkentensis*. It is so new, and so unusual, it has not yet got a commonly accepted English name. I call it the **Soviet Tree**. It was developed by scientists in the 1960s in what was then the Soviet Union – now Uzbekistan – by crossing two American species: **Indian Bean Tree** (see page 62) and **Desert Willow** (*Chilopsis linearis*). As these species are from different genera an 'x', denoting hybridity, appears at the beginning of the Latin name. If the tree was produced from species in the same genus, the 'x' would appear between the genus and species names.

The **Bee-Bee Tree** (*Tetradium daniellii*) is a very promising small tree from Korea. It has flower bunches in late summer which develop into brownish red berries. It is handsome in an understated way and appears to be quite happy on the street in the few (Hackney) sites where it can be found.

As its name suggests, those flowers act as a bee magnet, so it promises to be good for biodiversity as well as useful for a street planter wanting to expand their palette.

A tree I expect great things of is the delightfully named **Kentucky Coffee Tree** (*Gymnocladus dioicia*). A North American species that thrives in some East Coast cities, it makes for a distinguished medium-large tree. Currently a rare tree in London, it is likely to increase in number. Identified by huge, doubly serrate leaves, it's nothing to write home about when young, but becomes stately as it matures. An avenue tree of the future.

The evergreen **Catalina Ironwood** (*Lyonothamnus floribundus*) is endangered in the wild, being confined to the Californian Channel Island of Catalina, and very rare on the streets of London. Just one example of this characterful tree, with unusual leaves and shaggy red-brown bark, can be seen – on Chelsea's street-tree hotspot of Wilbraham Place. It deserves to be more widely planted.

Right above: The distinctive leaves of a Kentucky Coffee Tree, Elderfield Road, Clapton

Far right above: Fruits ripening in the canopy of a Bee-Bee Tree, Bouverie Road, Stoke Newington

Right below: A flowering Soviet Tree on Almington Street, Finsbury Park

Far right below: The Catalina Ironwood on Wilbraham Place, Chelsea

LONDON STREET TREE WALKS

Over the next few pages are six street tree trails in North, South, East and West London, the West End and the City. These trails will, I hope, give explorers an idea of the interest and diversity of our urban forest. Of course, in most parts of London you need only do a circuit of your own neighbourhood to see London's streets in a whole new light.

Picture: Raywood Ash trees, Druce Road, Dulwich

I. NORTH LONDON: AN ARCHWAY PERAMBULATION

This fairly long circular walk, centred on Archway Tube station, is full of surprises.

Take the Junction Road exit from the station. Immediately cross the road, noting newly planted Stone Pines and Southern Magnolias (**1**) on a traffic island, and Japanese Pagoda Trees, a Handkerchief Tree and a pink-flowering Magnolia (**2**) among new trees on the pedestrianised area next to the Archway Tower.

Turn right on the south side of Junction Road until you reach the St John's Tavern. Here turn left into St John's Grove, noting the Crimean Lime (**3**) outside the pub. Continue until you reach Pemberton Gardens and a pair of Dawn Redwoods (**4**). Continue to Holloway Road, which you will need to cross.

Turn left and then right into St John's Villas, where you can find eight Sand Pears (**5**) – look out for their large apple-like fruits in the autumn. At the end of St John's Villas turn left on Ashbrook Road, continuing to the junction with St John's Way. Follow this road to the right for a short distance, and turn left into Prospero Road.

Continue up Prospero Road admiring the **'Plena'** Wild Cherries (**6**), turning right at the end into Parrolles Road, which shortly becomes Cressida Road. Notice a fine pair of London Planes (**7**) opposite the Village Garage. Take the right turn into into Dresden Road (**8**), a street-tree hotspot. Look out for the Handkerchief Tree, Judas Tree, Crêpe Myrtle and Three-Lobed Apple or Bragania among many interesting trees on this street.

Halfway along this street turn into Ashmount Road and then left on Gladsmuir Road. You can find a **'Royal Burgundy'** Cherry and more Judas Trees (**9**) on this road. At the end, turn left and then right into Gladsmuir Road, lined primarily with Common Limes

(**10**). At the end of this street you come to Pauntley Street, with Chinese Lacebark Elms, a Raywood Ash and a Hop Hornbeam (**11**).

Now cross the busy Archway Road and head down Despard Road, where some mature white-berried Kashmiri Rowans can be seen (**12**). Turn left at the end of the road down Highgate Hill, cross over this road and turn right into Magdala Avenue opposite the main entrance to the Whittington Hospital.

This street is lined with several more Lacebark Elms (**13**), including the UK Champion Tree (the tallest example of the species in the country), among a selection of interesting trees. Note Turkish Hazel, a **'Laciniata'** Alder, and a couple of rare Yunnan Crabs.

At the end of this street, turn left onto Dartmouth Park Hill and, shortly afterwards, take a left into Bredgar Road, with yet another, unidentified, Elm (**14**). Turn left on Junction Road and retrace your steps to Archway Station.

Above: A Yunnan Apple on Magdala Avenue

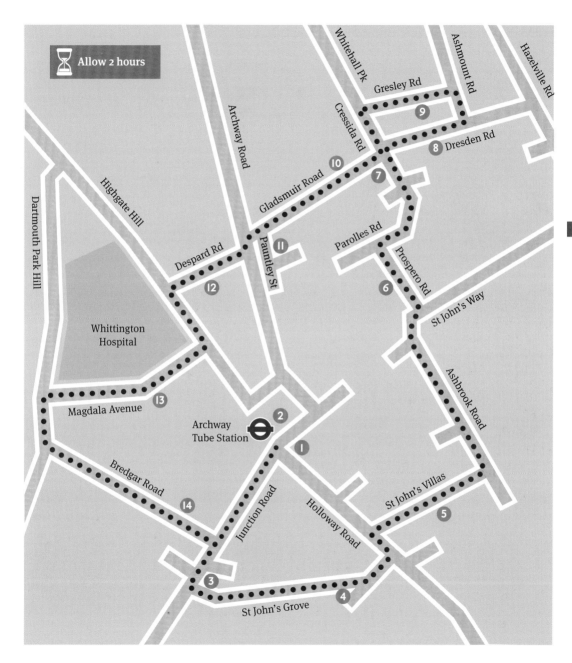

2. SOUTH LONDON: HERNE HILL HIGHLIGHTS

Particularly good in mid- late-March, this circular walk from Herne Hill Station, taking in two boroughs – Southwark and Lambeth – is designed for lovers of blossom, which is at its best in early spring.

Turn left out of Herne Hill mainline station onto Railton Road, noting **'Chanticleer'** Pears **(1)** lining this pedestrianised shopping area. Turn left under the railway bridge onto Half Moon Lane, taking the first right after the Half Moon pub and a Chang's Sweetgum **(2)** into Stradella Road.

On its west (right-hand) side, this street is lined with Yoshino Cherries **(3)**, with a mix of other species on the east side including a Silver Maple and a **'Beech Hill'** Pear **(4)**. Follow the road round at the end, and take the next left on the parallel Winterbrook Road, a consistent avenue of lovely Yoshinos **(5)**, at their best in the second half of March.

Turn right, back onto Half Moon Lane, noting a young **'New Horizon'** Elm **(6)** and an American Sweetgum **(7)**. Continue straight until you turn left into Beckwith Road, marked by a Holm Oak **(8)**. This street is traditionally planted with mature birches, including some good Silver Birches **(9)** and at least one Erman's Birch. Also note a mature **'Nigra'** Cherry Plum **(10)** and a Hibiscus **(11)**.

At the end of Beckwith Road turn left briefly onto Red Post Hill, noting a Turkish Hazel **(12)**. At the roundabout turn into Sunray Avenue, taking the next left into Casino Avenue, Herne Hill's Magnolia hotspot. Coinciding with the Yoshino Cherries, these will be at their best in the second half of March. Look out for the deep-pink-flowered **'Galaxy' (13)** cultivar and the more numerous white-flowered trees.

Continue along Casino Avenue, noting Indian Horse Chestnuts planted at the entrance to one cul-de-sac **(14)**, and a Dawn Redwood on the next. On the corner where Casino Avenue joins Herne Hill there is a small Olive tree **(15)**.

Here cross over the main road, and into the borough of Lambeth. Turn briefly right, and take the next left into Poplar Walk, lined with mature Ash trees **(16)**.

At the end of this street, take a left into Fawnbrake Avenue, planted with a good mix of species. Of particular note are an Amur Maple **(17)**, at least two Peanut Butter Trees **(18)** and a **'Soviet Tree' (19)**. Other trees present include various cherries, birches, mature **'Brilliantissimum'** Sycamores and some Juneberries.

Take a left at the end of Fawnbrake Avenue, and then turn left again into Gubyon Avenue, noting some fine **'Kanzan'** cherries **(20)**. Take the next right into Shardcroft Avenue briefly, and then turn left into Milkwood Road.

Continue down this sparsely planted street until you reach a pair of Whitebeams **(21)** marking the rear entrance to Herne Hill Station.

Above: Yoshino Cherry blossom on Stradella Road

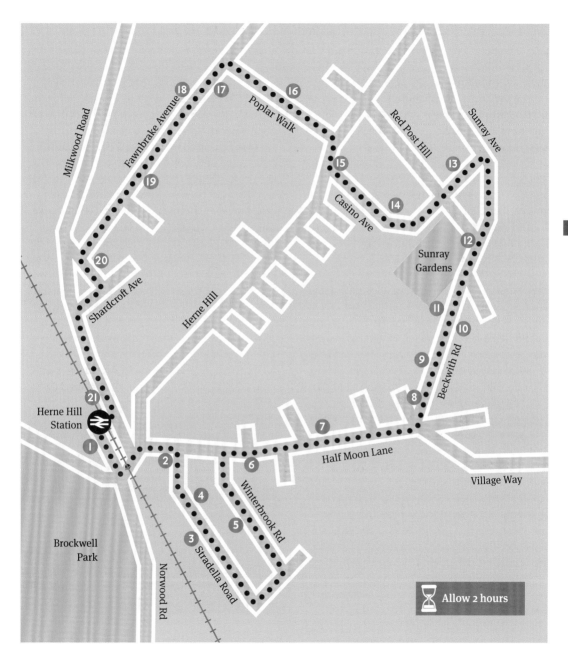

Milkwood Road

18 17 16

Fawnbrake Avenue

Poplar Walk

Red Post Hill

Sunray Ave

13

19

15

Casino Ave

14

12

20

Sunray Gardens

Shardcroft Ave

Herne Hill

11

10

9

8

Beckwith Rd

21

Herne Hill Station

7

Half Moon Lane

Village Way

1

2

6

Winterbrook Rd

4

5

3

Brockwell Park

Stradella Road

Norwood Rd

⏳ Allow 2 hours

3. EAST LONDON: THE HAGGERSTON HOP

A short circular walk centred on Haggerston Overground station, highlighting Hackney's remarkable arboreal diversity.

Outside Haggerston Station to your left you will notice a pair of maples: a small Field Maple and, to set the tone, a larger, and very unusual Trident Maple (**1**).

Having examined the maples, you will need to turn right out of the station on Lee Street under the railway, and then right onto Kingsland Road, walking past Arbutus Street, home to two Strawberry Trees (**2**).

Cross Kingsland Road and take a left on Downham Road, noting several Persian Ironwoods on either side of the street (**3**), some rocketing Dawn Redwoods (**4**) and a Japanese Pagoda Tree (**5**), marking the left hand turn into Hertford Road. Smaller Dawn Redwoods, a Turkish Hazel and some Sweetgums line this most un-crescent-like street. As it turns a corner into De Beauvoir Crescent notice a **'Dalecarnica'** cut-leaved Silver Birch (**6**), and examples of both the **'Laciniata'** and **'Imperialis'** cultivars of the common Alder (**7**).

At the end of this street, turn right into De Beauvoir Road, planted with a range of trees. Once you cross Downham Road there are some trees of note: a couple of Nettle Trees and a young Tulip Tree (**8**), another Persian Ironwood (**9**), an Almond outside the David Adjaye-designed 'Sunken House' at 75a (**10**), and an **'Amber Beauty'** Manchurian Cherry (**11**).

Beyond the mini-roundabout at the end of this street you will notice a mature fastigiate Hornbeam and a Yoshino Cherry (**12**).

Turn right into Englefield Road and then right again into Mortimer Road, noting a Juneberry (**13**) on your right.

Now skirt round the north and east sides of De Beauvoir Square to its south-east corner, where you

turn left into St. Peter's Way. On this street you will see a very large Italian Alder and a young Wild Service Tree (**14**).

At the end of this street you will need to cross back over Kingsland Road, and head under the railway bridge on Middleton Road, just after which you will see a **'Forest Pansy'** Eastern Redbud (**15**) on your right. Continue straight ahead, passing a Chonosuki Crab Apple and a River Birch (**16**), and then turn right into Holly Street, not yet lined with hollies...

Where this street meets Albion Square, two mature Tree of Heaven (**17**) specimens block the road. Walk round Albion Square and out on to Haggerston Road in the south-west corner, where you will see a mature Purple Crab Apple and a Hornbeam (**18**).

From here, you can cross the road and walk back to Lee Street through Stonebridge Gardens, walking past the Trident Maple next to the station entrance.

Above: The Trident Maple outside Haggerston Station

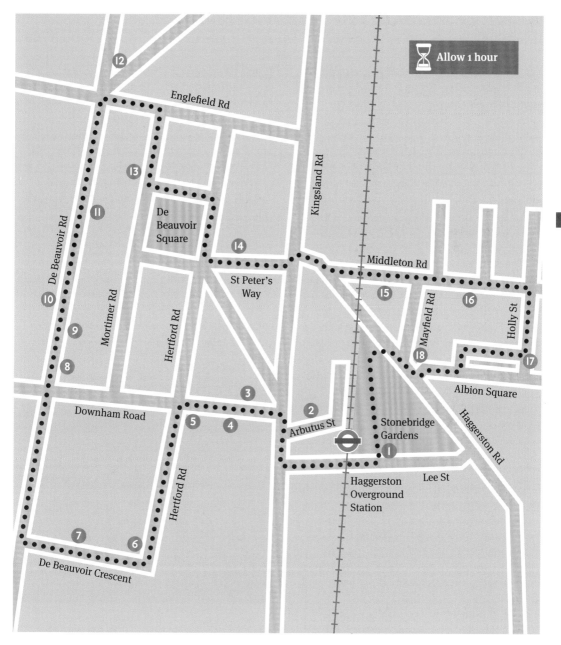

Allow 1 hour

Englefield Rd

Kingsland Rd

De Beauvoir Rd

De Beauvoir Square

Mortimer Rd

Hertford Rd

St Peter's Way

Middleton Rd

Mayfield Rd

Holly St

Downham Road

Hertford Rd

Arbutus St

Stonebridge Gardens

Albion Square

Haggerston Rd

Lee St

Haggerston Overground Station

De Beauvoir Crescent

4. WEST LONDON: STEVE'S CHISWICK CHASE

This walk was inspired by Steve Pocock, who guided me round the streets of Chiswick, where we discovered all manner of unusual trees.

Turn left out of Turnham Green Tube station on Turnham Green Terrace until you reach Chiswick High Road, which you should cross. Turn right and continue for a short distance until you turn off left into Devonshire Road, planted with **'Chanticleer'** pears **(1)**

At the corner of Glebe Street you will see a good example of a mature Raywood Ash **(2)** along with some neatly maintained Common Limes **(3)**. Turn right into Glebe Street, and then left on to Duke Road, admiring the Norway Maples; you will double back on yourself along Binns Road, where among the Winter Flowering Cherries a Japanese Zelkova **(4)** has snuck in. In summer this has very similar leaves, but it is a much larger tree than the cherries, so my hunch is this tree was a mistake!

After Binns Road you will be zig-zagging back along the next two parallel streets. Look out for the Honey Locust **(5)** on Dale Street before turning into Reckitt Road, planted with several Golden Rain Trees, including one particularly large specimen **(6)**. On Quick Road look out for the Ginkgos **(7)**.

At the end of this street, turn right, but do look at another pair of fine Raywood Ash trees **(8)** behind you on Dale Street. Next turn left on Wood Street, at the end of which is a very large Oriental Plane **(9)**.

Now for a little dog-leg onto Ashbourne Grove, lined with fastigiate Hornbeams **(10)**; then take a right onto Eastbury Grove – a whole street of Hybrid Cockspur Thorns **(11)**. Turn left onto Cornwall Grove, halfway along which is a Rowan tree with Mistletoe **(12)** growing in it – much easier to see in winter.

At the end of this street turn left into Chiswick Lane, admiring a Holm Oak in Homefield Rec on your right. Turn off right down Beverley Road, where you will find a mature Copper Beech **(13)** along with some fine mature Field Maples. Turn off left down Airedale Avenue, admiring the Silver Birches, among which you will find an unusual River Birch **(14)**.

At the end of Airedale Road you should turn left back onto Chiswick High Road. Prominent along this mostly Plane-lined street is a **'Glauca'** Atlas Cedar (*Cedrus atlantica*) **(15)**, at the corner with Chiswick Lane.

Above: The Cornwall Grove Rowan hosts Mistletoe

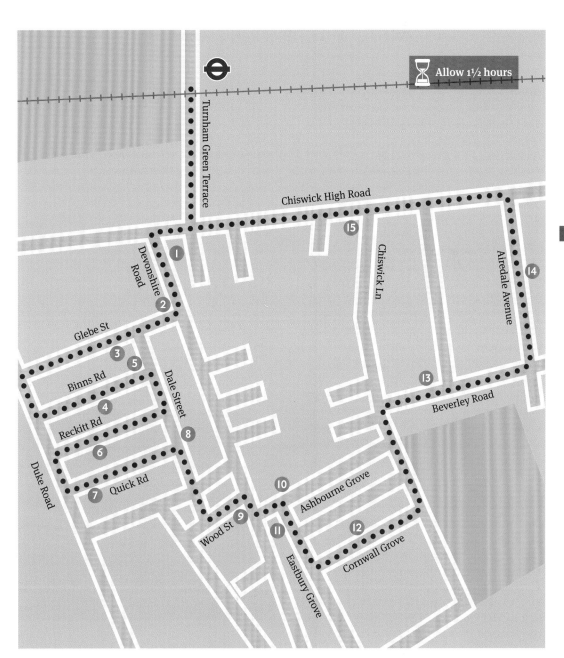

Allow 1½ hours

Turnham Green Terrace

Chiswick High Road

Devonshire Road

Chiswick Ln

Airedale Avenue

15

1

2

Glebe St

3

5

Binns Rd

Dale Street

4

Reckitt Rd

8

13

Beverley Road

6

Duke Road

Quick Rd

7

10

Ashbourne Grove

Wood St

9

11

Eastbury Grove

12

Cornwall Grove

14

5. WEST END: A BLOOMSBURY & FITZROVIA JAUNT

This walk takes you into Bloomsbury and Fitzrovia, two quite distinct areas of London, and, while most lies in the Borough of Camden, it nips briefly into the City of Westminster too.

On exiting Goodge Street Tube station, turn left on Tottenham Court Road. The first tree to admire is a young Elm, probably a **'New Horizon'** cultivar **(1)**, on the corner of Tottenham Street. Continue straight on under the canopy of mature London Plane trees until you reach the pedestrian crossing beyond the American Church. Take a moment to admire the rather corpulent, rough-barked Plane tree **(2)**, a **'Pyramidalis'** cultivar, behind you.

Across the road, head down Torrington Place where there are more, younger Planes. Keep straight on, crossing Gower Street to admire yet another Plane **(3)** outside Waterstones. This one was voted a Great Tree of London, and is interesting to compare with the **'Pyramidalis'**.

As Torrington Place becomes Byng Place, the trees change. On the south side a pair of One-leaved Ash trees **(4)** – a Camden favourite – are accompanied by a graceful Raywood Ash **(5)** over on the north.

Beyond Malet Street, half a dozen Japanese Pagoda Trees **(6)** line the street, before we turn right onto Torrington Square by a fine Sycamore **(7)**. Head straight down through the UCL campus past an American Sweetgum **(8)** and a Cappadocian Maple **(9)**, and past the magnificent Planes, including at least one potential Oriental Plane **(10)** on your right.

At the end, turn right past SOAS, exiting through the gates onto Malet Street, where you turn left and, opposite Senate House, right onto Keppel Street, where you will find a Rowan **(11)**, a pair of mature Whitebeams **(12)** and, just before the corner with

Gower Street, a Wild Service Tree **(13)**.

Turn left on to treeless Gower Street and then right onto Bedford Square, where some of the oldest and most enormous Planes **(14)** on this route can be seen. Skirt the northern side of the square to emerge via Bayley Street onto Tottenham Court Road, which you must cross to see the Italian Alders **(15)** on the corner of Percy Street.

Head down Percy Street admiring the False Acacias **(16)**, before crossing into Westminster where a male and female pair of Ginkgos **(17)** – a Westminster favourite – stand guard outside the Marquis of Granby.

Follow Rathbone Street round to Charlotte Street, passing a Chonosuki Crab Apple outside the Duke of York. As you turn left onto Charlotte Street a purple-leaved Sycamore **(18)** signals your re-emergence in Camden, and is followed by a Norway Maple **(19)**.

Turn right onto Goodge Street, lined with Field Maples **(20)**, and then left onto Tottenham Court Road to return to the Tube station.

Above: The purple-leaved Sycamore on Charlotte Street

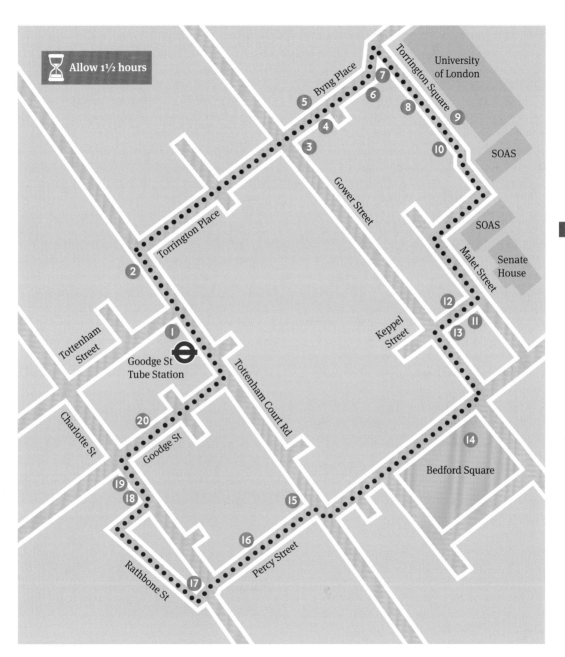

Allow 1½ hours

University of London

Torrington Square

Byng Place

5

4

3

7

6

8

9

10

SOAS

SOAS

Senate House

Malet Street

Gower Street

Torrington Place

2

Keppel Street

12

13

11

Tottenham Street

1

Goodge St Tube Station

Tottenham Court Rd

14

Bedford Square

20

Goodge St

15

Charlotte St

19

18

16

Percy Street

Rathbone St

17

6. THE CITY: A SQUARE MILE SAUNTER

Not only are there trees of great interest on this walk, but it takes you past some of the City's most spectacular skyscrapers. It is best on a weekend morning when the crowds, and the traffic, will be less oppressive.

Leaving Bank Station at Exit One, you emerge on the corner of Mansion House Street and Princes Street. Head west keeping the postmodern No 1 Poultry to your left. Our first tree is an American Sweetgum **(1)** on the corner of Cheapside and King Street.

Cross Cheapside and make for the unusual Spaeth's Alder **(2)** outside Daunt Books. Next, turn left into Bow Lane. Head straight over Watling Street, passing St Mary Aldermary and its fine Oriental Plane **(3)**, before emerging at a junction where you head east down Cannon Street.

After a trio of London Planes **(4)** outside the Bloomberg Building, cross the road and continue along Cannon Street, stopping for a **'New Horizon'** Elm **(5)** outside Boots, and a tenacious pair of White-beams **(6)** guarding 110. From here, head straight along to the busy intersection at the northern end of London Bridge, and continue east along Eastcheap.

On the south side of Eastcheap, just before Lovat Lane, stands a False Acacia **(7)**; a little further along, enjoy the view down St Mary at Hill to a handsome mature Italian Alder **(8)** at its southern end. Across the road, a fine Common Lime **(9)** outside St Margaret Pattens church marks the entrance to Rood Lane, where you head north to the Walkie-Talkie. Various trees have been planted around its base, most prominently fastigiate Elms, maybe of the **'Columella'** cultivar **(10)**.

At the end of Rood Lane, turn left onto Fenchurch Street and then right onto treeless Lime Street, which curves round until it becomes pedestrianised. Newly planted London Planes **(11)** stand between the Lloyds Building and the Willis Towers. Beyond these are Leadenhall Street and the Cheesegrater, with its fastigiate Southern Magnolias **(12)**.

Crossing Leadenhall Street, turn left before turning left down St Mary Axe to the Gherkin, with its surrounding Dawn Redwoods **(13)**. Continue straight until you reach busy Camomile Street, where you turn left.

Turn left again into Bishopsgate, passing pleached Hornbeams **(14)** on Clerk's Place next to St Ethelburga's Church. Across the road stands a solitary Ginkgo **(15)**, but continue on the south side, past the bulk of 22 Bishopsgate, until you reach the junction with Threadneedle Street.

At the next junction just beyond them, turn right into Cornhill, which leads back to Bank Station. This barren street is softened only by the Small-leaved Limes **(16)** tucked away next to the Royal Exchange.

Above: Needle-less Dawn Redwoods around the Gherkin

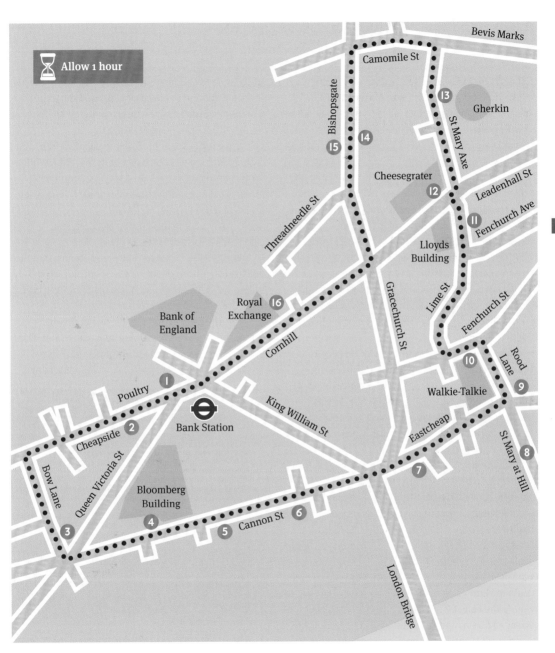

Allow 1 hour

Bevis Marks

Camomile St

Bishopsgate

Gherkin

13

St Mary Axe

15   14

Cheesegrater

Threadneedle St

12

Leadenhall St

11   Fenchurch Ave

Lloyds
Building

Royal
Exchange   16

Bank of
England

Gracechurch St

Lime St

Fenchurch St

Cornhill

1

Fenchurch St

Poultry

10

Rood
Lane

Cheapside

2

Bank Station

King William St

Walkie-Talkie

9

Bow Lane

Queen Victoria St

Bloomberg
Building

Eastcheap

St Mary at Hill

8

4

5   Cannon St   6

7

3

London Bridge

INDEX OF LATIN NAMES

Abies x borisii-regis 179

Acacia dealbata. 14

Acca sellowiana 18

Acer buergarianum. 20

Acer campestre 22

Acer cappadocicum 21

Acer davidii 20

Acer x freemanii 21

Acer ginnala 21

Acer griseum 20

Acer negundo 21

Acer platanoides. 24

Acer pseudoplatanus 26

Acer rubrum 21

Acer saccharinum. 20

Acer saccharum 21

Aesculus flava 30

Aesculus x carnea. 30

Aesculus hippocastanum 32

Aesculus indica. 30

Ailanthus altissima 34

Albizia julibrissin 38

Alnus cordata 42

Alnus glutinosa. 40

Alnus incana 40

Alnus x spaethii 40

Amelanchier arborea 46

Araucaria heterophylla 179

Arbutus x andrachnoides 49, 142

Arbutus unedo 48

Betula albosinensis 52

Betula ermanii 52

Betula maximowicziana 52

Betula nigra. 52

Betula papyrifera 53

Betula pubescens 53

Betula pendula 54

Betula sichuanensis 53

Betula utilis var. jacquemontii 56

Brousonettia papyrifera. 130

Callistemon citrinus 16

Carpinus betulus. 58

Carpinus japonica. 58

Castanea sativa 60

Catalpa bignonioides 58

Cedrus atlantica 140

Cedrus deodara. 140, 176

Cedrus libani 140

Celtis australis. 66

Cercis canadensis 68

Cercis silliquastrum 68

Chilopsis linearis 68

x Chitalpa tashkentensis 204

Citrus x limon 178

Clerodendrum trichotomum 70

Cordyline australis 72, 142

Cornus controversa. 74

Cornus kousa. 74

Cornus mas 74

Corylus colurna. 76

Crataegus crus-galli 78

Crataegus laevigata 80

Crataegus monogyna 80

Crataegus pedicellata. 78

Crataegus persimilis. 78

Crataegus prunifolia. 78

Crataegus x lavalleei 78

Cupressus sempervirens 142

Davidia involucrata 84

Diospyros kaki 109

Eriolobus trilobatus 86

Eucalyptus gunnii 14

Fagus sylvatica 88, 142

Fraxinus angustifolia 94

Fraxinus excelsior 92

Fraxinus ornus 92

Fraxinus pennsylvanica. 92

Ginkgo biloba 96

Gleditsia tricanthos 98

Gymnocladus dioicus. 191

Hibiscus syriacus 100

Hibiscus 'Resi'. 100

Hippophae salicifolia. 104

Hoheria sexstylosa 142

Jacaranda mimosifolia. 181

Koelreuteria paniculata 106

Lagerstroemia indica 110

Larix decidua 140

Ligustrum lucidum. 112

Liquidambar acalycina 114

Liquidambar styraciflua 114

Liriodendron tulipifera 116

Lophostemon confertus. 179

Lyonothamnus floribundus. 193

Magnolia 'Galaxy'. 118

Magnolia grandiflora 121

Magnolia kobus 121

Magnolia x loebneri 121

Magnolia x soulangeana 118

Malus 'Adirondack'. 125

Malus 'Evereste' 122

Malus floribunda 125

Malus 'Golden Hornet'. 125

Malus 'John Downie' 125

Malus 'Profusion' 125

Malus x purpurea 125

Malus 'Rudolph' 125

Malus 'Street Parade' 125

Malus trilobata 86

Malus tschonoskii. 122

Malus yunnanensis 125

Metasequoia glyptostroboides . . . 128
Metrosideros excelsa 179
Morus alba. 130
Morus nigra 130
Olea europaea. 132
Ostrya carpinifolia 134
Parrotia persica. 136
Paulownia tomentosa 138
Pinus nigra 140
Pinus pinea 140, 142
Pinus radiata. 140
Pinus sylvestris 140
Platanus x acerifolia. 144
Platanus x hispanica 144
Platanus occidentalis. 144
Platanus orientalis 148
Populus nigra 152
Populus nigra 'Italica' 152
Populus tremula 152
Populus x canadensis 152
Populus x canescens 152
Prunus 'Amanagawa' 157
Prunus x amygdalo-persica. 154
Prunus avium 154
Prunus cerasifera 154
Prunus dulcis 154
Prunus x hillieri 'Spire' 157
Prunus 'Kanzan' 154
Prunus maackii. 157
Prunus padus 154
Prunus 'Royal Burgundy' 157
Prunus x subhirtella. 154
Prunus 'Tai Haku'. 157
Prunus x yedoensis 154
Pseudopanax crassifolius 142
Pterocarya fraxinifolia. 164
Pyrus calleryana. 168

Pyrus communis. 166
Pyrus pyrifolia. 109, 166
Pyrus salicifolia 166
Quercus cerris 170
Quercus coccinea 170
Quercus frainetto 179
Quercus x hispanica. 170
Quercus ilex. 170
Quercus palustris 170
Quercus petrea 172
Quercus robur 172
Quercus rubra 170
Quercus suber 170
Robinia pseudoacacia 174
Salix fragilis. 182
Salix matsudana. 182
Salix x sepulcralis 182
Schinus molle 109, 179
Sequoia sempervirens 176
Sequoiadendron giganteum 176
Sophora japonica 194
Sorbus aria. 186
Sorbus aucuparia 188
Sorbus commixta 184
Sorbus domestica 179
Sorbus x intermedia. 184
Sorbus latifola 184
Sorbus torminalis 190
Sorbus x thuringiaca 184
Styphnolobium japonicum 194
Taxodium distichum 128
Tetradium daniellii. 204
Tilia cordata. 196
Tilia x europaea 198
Tilia henryana 196
Tilia mongolica 196
Tilia platyphyllos 196

Tilia tomentosa 196
Trachycarpus fortunei 72
Ulmus americana 200
Ulmus x hollandica 200
Ulmus laevis 198
Ulmus 'Lutece' 200
Ulmus 'New Horizon'. 200
Ulmus parvifolia. 200
Ulmus x hollandica 200
Zelkova carpinifolia 202
Zelkova serrata 202

INDEX OF COMMON NAMES

Acacia, False 174
Alder, European 40
Alder, Grey 40
Alder, Italian 42
Alder, Spaeth's 40
Almond 154
Ash, Green 92
Ash, Golden 92
Ash, Manna 92
Ash, Mountain 186
Ash, One-leaved 92
Ash, 'Raywood' 94
Aspen 152
Bean Tree, Indian 62
Bee-Bee Tree 204
Beech 142
Beech, Copper 88
Birch, Chinese Red 52
Birch, Downy 53
Birch, Erman's 52
Birch, Himalayan 56
Birch, Monarch 52
Birch, Paper 53
Birch, River 52
Birch, Sichuan 53
Birch, Silver 54
Bottlebrush Tree 16
Box, Brisbane 179
Box Elder 20
Bragania 86
Buckeye, Yellow 30
Cabbage Tree 72, 142
Catalpa, Southern 62
Cedar, Atlas 140
Cedar, Deodar 140, 176
Cedar of Lebanon 140
Cherry Plum, Black 154

Cherry, 'Accolade' 154
Cherry, Bird 157
Cherry, Cornelian 74
Cherry, Flagpole 157
Cherry, 'Great White' 157
Cherry, 'Kanzan' 157
Cherry, Manchurian 157
Cherry, 'Royal Burgundy' 157
Cherry, 'Snow Goose' 154
Cherry, 'Spire' 157
Cherry, 'Tai Haku' 157
Cherry, 'Okame' 154
Cherry, 'Umineko' 154
Cherry, Wild 154
Cherry, Winter-Flowering 154
Cherry, Yoshino 154
Chestnut, Sweet 60
Christmas Tree, New Zealand 179
Coffee Tree, Kentucky 204
Crab Apple, 'Adirondack' 125
Crab Apple, Chonosuki 122
Crab Apple, Erect 86
Crab Apple, 'Evereste' 122
Crab Apple, 'Golden Hornet' 125
Crab Apple, Japanese 125
Crab Apple, 'John Downie' 125
Crab Apple, 'Profusion' 125
Crab Apple, Purple 125
Crab Apple, 'Rudolph' 125
Crab Apple, Street Parade 125
Crab Apple, Yunnan 125
Cypress, Italian 142
Cypress, Swamp 128
Dogwood, Chinese 74
Dove Tree 84
Elm, Chinese Lacebark 200
Elm, European White 200

Elm, Golden 200
Elm, 'Lutece' 200
Elm, Huntingdon 200
Elm, 'New Horizon' 200
Elm, Princeton 200
Feijoa 18
Fir, Macedonian 179
Foxglove Tree 138
Gean 154
Ginkgo 96
Golden Rain Tree 106
Glorybower, Harlequin 70
Guava, Pineapple 18
Gum, Tasmanian Cider 14
Handkerchief Tree 84
Haw, Scarlet 78
Hawthorn, 'Paul's Scarlet' 80
Hawthorn, 'Stricta' 80
Hazel, Turkish 76
Hibiscus 100
Hornbeam 58
Hornbeam, Hop 134
Hornbeam, Japanese 58
Horse Chestnut 32
Horse Chestnut, Indian 30
Horse Chestnut, Red 30
Ironwood, Catalina 204
Ironwood, Persian 136
Jacaranda 181
Judas Tree 68
Juneberry 46
Keyaki 202
Lacebark, New Zealand 142
Lancewood 142
Larch, European 140
Lemon 178
Lime, Common 198

Lime, Henry's 196
Lime, Large-Leaved 196
Lime, Mongolian. 196
Lime, Silver 196
Lime, Small-leaved. 196
Locust, Black. 174
Locust, Honey 98
Magnolia, 'Galaxy' 118
Magnolia, Hybrid 121
Magnolia, Kobushi 121
Magnolia, 'Merrill' 121
Magnolia, Southern 121
Magnolia, Saucer 118
Magnolia, 'Yellow Bird' 118
Maple, Amur 21
Maple, Cappadocian 21
Maple, Field. 22
Maple, Freeman's 21
Maple, Norway 24
Maple, Paperbark 20
Maple, Père David's 20
Maple, Silver 20
Maple, Trident 20
Maple, Red. 21
Mespil, Snowy. 46
Mimosa. 14
Mulberry, Paper 130
Mulberry, Black. 130
Mulberry, White 130
Myrtle, Crêpe. 110
Nettle Tree 66
Oak, Cork 170
Oak, English 172
Oak, Fulham 170
Oak, Holm 170
Oak, Hungarian. 178
Oak, Pin 170

Oak, Red. 170
Oak, Scarlet 170
Oak, Sessile 172
Oak, Turkey 170
Olive 132
Pagoda Tree, Japanese 194
Palm, Cabbage 72
Palm, Chusan 72
Peanut Butter Tree 70
Peach, Hybrid 154
Pear, 'Beech Hill'. 66
Pear, 'Bradford' 168
Pear, 'Chanticleer'. 168
Pear, Sand 109, 166
Pear, Weeping 166
Persimmon. 109
Pepper Tree, Peruvian 109, 179
Pine, Austrian 140
Pine, Monterey 140
Pine, Norfolk Island 179
Pine, Scots 140
Pine, Stone. 140
Plane, London. 144
Plane, Oriental 148
Plum, Cherry 154
Pohutukawa 179
Poplar, Black. 152
Poplar, Grey. 152
Poplar, Hybrid Black 152
Poplar, Lombardy 152
Princess Tree 138
Privet, Chinese Tree 112
Redbud, 'Forest Pansy' 68
Redwood, Coast 176
Redwood, Dawn 128
Redwood, Giant 176
Rowan 188

Rowan, Chinese Scarlet 184
Sandthorn, Willow-leaved. 104
Service Tree, Bastard 184
Service Tree of Fontainebleau. . . . 184
Service Tree, True 179
Service Tree, Wild. 190
Shadbush. 46
Silk Tree, Persian 38
'Soviet Tree'. 204
Strawberry Tree. 48
Strawberry Tree, Hybrid. 48, 142
Sweetgum, American 114
Sweetgum, Chang's 114
Sycamore 26
Sycamore, American 144
Thorn, Broad-Leaved Cockspur . . . 78
Thorn, Cockspur 78
Thorn, Frosted. 78
Thorn, Hybrid Cockspur 78
Tree of Heaven. 34
Tulip Tree. 116
Wattle, Silver. 14
Wedding Cake Tree. 74
Willow, Corkscrew 182
Willow, Crack 182
Willow, Desert. 204
Willow, Weeping. 182
Whitebeam 186
Whitebeam, Swedish 184
Wingnut, Caucasian. 164
Zelkova, Caucasian. 202
Zelkova, Japanese. 202

FURTHER READING

If, after reading this book, you would like to read more about the themes discussed in it, here are some pointers:

Chadbund, Geoffrey, *Flowering Cherries* (First edition). London: Collins, 1972

Gilbert, Bob, *Ghost Trees: Nature and People in a London Parish* (First edition). Salford: Saraband, 2018

Johnson, Owen and More, David, *Collins Tree Guide* (Paperback editon). London: HarperCollins, 2006

Johnston, Mark, *Street Trees in Britain* (First edition). Oxford: Windgather Press, 2017

Johnston, Mark, *Trees in Towns and Cities* (First edition). Oxford: Windgather Press, 2015

Landreth, Jenny, *The Great Trees of London* (First edition). London: Time Out Guides Ltd, 2010

Taylor, Graham, *Ada Salter: Pioneer of Ethical Socialism* (First edition). London: Lawrence and Wishart, 2016

Tudge, Colin, *The Secret Life of Trees: How They Live and Why They Matter* (Paperback edition). London: Penguin, 2006

Webster, A. D., *London Trees*. London: Swarthmore Press, 1920

USEFUL WEBSITES

Barcham Trees: **barchampro.co.uk**
Deptford Folk: **deptfordfolk.org**
Forestry Commission, London iTree eco project:
    forestry.gov.uk/london-itree
Hillier: **hillier.co.uk/trees**
London National Park City: **nationalparkcity.london**
London Tree Officers Association: **ltoa.org.uk**
London Wildlife Trust: **wildlondon.org.uk**
Mayor of London's Street Trees map:
    maps.london.gov.uk/trees/
Street Trees for Living: **streettreesforliving.org**

Saunders Seasonings: **sauders-seasonings.co.uk**
The Tree Council: **treecouncil.org.uk**
Trees & Design Action Group: **tdag.org.uk**
Trees for Cities: **treesforcities.org**
Urban Tree Festival: **urbantreefestival.org**
Woodland Trust: **woodlandtrust.org.uk**
Street tree trails are mapped on several digital guides including Go Jauntly, **gojauntly.com**, TiCL, **ticl.me**; and TreeTalk, **treetalk.co.uk**

PICTURE CREDITS

28	© The National Gallery, London. Bequeathed by Lord Astor of Hever, 1971
29	Mark Johnston
39	(top left) Graham Coster
64	Dave Higgens/PA
65	Susan Unwin
90	Alamy
91	(bottom) R. Wesley, Hulton Archive/Getty Images
102	Regular Cleaning
146	(top) © Museum of London
147	Michael J Keane
151	© Wolf Suschitzky/Museum of London
160	© The National Gallery, London
161	© The National Gallery, London.
162	© Keith Coventry, courtesy of Pace Gallery
163	Leeds Museums and Galleries (Leeds Art Gallery) UK/Bridgeman Images
169	(top left) Mira Bajagic
178	Alamy
179	(top right) Tomas del Amo/Alamy Stock Photo
180-1	DiscoverBA/Alamy
199	(bottom left) David Gee 1/Alamy

All other photos © Paul Wood